Cooking
with
Friends

Terri Grimes

DM Productions * Indiana

Cooking with Friends

Complete Guide to our very Favorite Foods

A DM Productions Publication/2007

Copyright 2007 by Terri Grimes

All rights reserved

Cover designed by Terri Grimes

Printed in The United States of America

ISBN: 978-0-6151-4860-1

Distributed by Lulu

http://www.lulu.com/content/856802

Acknowledgements

Many thanks to all who have sent recipes and stories to be included in this book. This book would not have been possible without each and every one of you.

Endless amounts of gratitude go to the Indy Writers Group for their feedback, advice and encouragement. Thanks go out to Kate Chaplin for creating the Indy Writers Group and special thanks to my favorite author, Debra Kemp, for not only inviting me to my first Indy Writers Group meeting, but also for giving me the belief that dreams can come true.

To my Greggy Bear, thanks for all the dinner dishes you washed while I sat glued to the computer writing. As my most devoted supporter and confidant, I affectionately dedicate this book to you.

Foreword

You could always count on Grandmom to have something good cooking in her kitchen. The lightest, fluffiest biscuits in the morning, succulent vegetables fresh from the garden for lunch and chicken fried steak and gravy for dinner that would melt in your mouth.

Grandmom could cook anything. And if you needed to know how to cook something, she was the one to ask. With love and patience she taught several generations how to cook.

For more than seventy-five years Grandmom cooked. She didn't write her recipes down, cooking from memory alone. Never would you find a measuring implement in her kitchen, it was always a pinch of this or a palm full of that. Grandmom cooked from the heart and her food reflected it. She was famous for stating that no one would ever leave her table hungry, and no one ever did.

Grandmom gave me the greatest gift of all, her love of cooking. She would place her weathered hands on my young smooth ones and guide me in kneading her famous biscuits. She taught me that she had lived through tough times in the depression years so food was to be treated with respect and not wasted.

I taught my daughter, Brooke, the lessons Grandmom taught me and now I am teaching my granddaughter, Jasmine, the same lessons. On a warm summers evening Jasmine and I will sit on the patio together, watching the fireflies and snapping garden fresh green beans, just as Grandmom and I had done so many years ago on the front porch. This cookbook is in honor of my Grandmom, Lottie Smith, and is a legacy for my daughter, Brooke Houk and granddaughter, Jasmine Timmons who have inherited Grandmom Lottie's love of cooking as well. These females are my heroes and are my heart. God Bless!

Contents

Appetizers

Atomic Buffalo Turds

B.L.T. Pizza

Buffalo Wings

Fresh Fruit Dip

Guacamole

Hot Crab Dip

Pineapple Papaya Salsa

Sassy Salsa

Sausage Balls

Smoked Beef Cheese Ball

Spicy Bean Dip

Spinach & Artichoke Dip

Tuna Mold

Zesty Cheese Straws

Atomic Buffalo Turds

Greg Grimes, Indianapolis Indiana

14 fresh Jalapenos　　　　　　　*7 bacon slices, halved*

One 8-ounce package cream cheese

Cut a slit in each jalapeno and remove seeds. Cut a ½-inch piece of cream cheese and stick inside of jalapeno. Wrap bacon piece around the jalapeno you just stuffed. Use toothpick to secure. Repeat until all jalapenos are stuffed and wrapped. Place jalapenos on grill, shut lid and cook over indirect heat until the bacon is done, about 20 or 30 minutes.

Yield 14 'Turds'

B.L.T. Pizza

Kate Chaplin, Indianapolis Indiana

Use a larger pizza crust for an easy and refreshing lunch or dinner! As a busy Wife, Mother, Author (The Belief Test) and emerging Film-Maker, fast and easy recipes are about all that fits into my hectic life these days.

One 8-inch ready made pizza crust　　*1 cup shredded mozzarella cheese*

1 teaspoon olive oil　　　　　　　*2 cups shredded lettuce*

½ teaspoon dry basil flakes　　　　*2 tablespoons mayonnaise*

¼ teaspoon garlic powder　　　　　*5 grape tomatoes*

¼ teaspoon onion powder　　　　　*1 tablespoon bacon bits*

Preheat oven to 425°F. Coat crust with oil. Sprinkle basil, garlic powder and onion powder on crust. Top with mozzarella. Bake 10 minutes or until cheese is melted. In a bowl, combine chopped lettuce, mayo, and bacon bits. When cheese is melted, cut pizza into sections. Top with lettuce mixture. Cut tomatoes in thirds, placing a few on each piece.

Serves 1 to 2

Buffalo Wings

Terri Grimes, Indianapolis Indiana

These wings are so awesome you will swear you are at the Anchor Bar in Buffalo New York.

½ cup red hot sauce (I prefer Franks)   *2 pounds chicken wings, trimmed*

1/3 cup butter

Deep fry wings in hot oil until crispy (approximately 7 to 10 minutes). Drain on paper towels. In medium saucepan combine hot sauce and butter. Heat until butter is melted. Toss wings with hot sauce and serve.
Serves 6 to 8

Fresh Fruit Dip

Cindy Newsom, Walker Louisiana

This dip is best made several hours earlier, or even the day before, so the flavors can meld and fully develop.

8-ounce cream cheese   *1 tablespoon Orange juice*

One 7-ounce jar marshmallow cream   *Dash Ginger*

1 tablespoon orange zest

Soften cream cheese. In medium mixing bowl combine all ingredients and mix well. Put in dip bowl and enjoy. Serve as accompaniment to fresh fruits.

Serves 4 to 6

Guacamole

Cindy Newsom, Walker Louisiana

Guacamole isn't just for topping enchiladas or burritos. Served with tortilla chips or celery sticks this dish makes a wonderful appetizer or late night snack.

3 medium avocados

1 tablespoon onions, minced

4 slices jalapeno peppers, minced

1 tablespoon lemon juice

2 tablespoon sour cream

Peel the avocados, remove seed and puree to a coarse, chunky texture. Mix onions, peppers, lemon juice and sour cream with avocados until well blended.

Serves 6 to 8

Hot Crab Dip

Terri Grimes, Indianapolis Indiana

Being originally from a coastal area of Maryland where blue crabs are abundant, I am happy to see blue crab meat at most seafood counters now. This dip is worth the expense of the crab and is impressive to serve to guests.

1 cup mayonnaise

1 ½ cups grated cheddar cheese

1 ½ teaspoons Old Bay seasoning

1 teaspoon Worcestershire sauce

¼ teaspoon yellow prepared mustard

1 pound fresh lump blue crab meat

Preheat oven to 350°F. Combine mayonnaise, ¾ cup cheese, old bay, Worcestershire sauce and mustard. Mix well. Gently fold in crab meat. Spoon mixture into 1 quart casserole dish. Top with remaining cheese. Sprinkle top with additional dash of old bay seasoning. Bake 15 minutes or until crab dip is hot and bubbly. Serve with crackers or tortilla chips.

Serves 4 to 6

Pineapple Papaya Salsa

Terri Grimes, Indianapolis Indiana

3 tomatoes

1 fresh pineapple

1 papaya

1 mango

1 bunch green onions, minced

¼ cup minced cilantro

2 jalapenos, seeded and minced

3 tablespoons fresh lemon juice

1 teaspoon finely minced garlic

2 teaspoons kosher salt

Core and dice tomatoes. Peel, core and dice pineapple. Peel, seed and dice papaya and mango. Add remaining ingredients; toss well. Chill one hour prior to serving. Serve with tortilla chips, or as a topping for cooked fish such as tilapia or swordfish. Yummy!

Yield 2 quarts

Sassy Salsa

Terri Grimes, Indianapolis Indiana

One 10-ounce can Rotel tomatoes (original)

Three 10-ounce cans Rotel tomatoes (mild)

1 cup crushed tomatoes

1/4 cup chopped green pepper

1/4 cup chopped yellow pepper

1 jalapeno, minced

1 mild banana pepper, minced

1 small bunch green onions, minced

1/4 cup red onion, minced

1/4 cup cilantro, minced

1 teaspoon garlic powder

1 teaspoon ground cumin

1 teaspoon kosher salt (optional)

Juice from 1 small lime

Juice from ½ lemon

Mix all of the ingredients together and stir well. Wait at least 1 hour before serving, so flavors have a chance to meld. Serve with tortilla chips.

Yield 1 ½ quarts

Sausage Balls

Terri Grimes, Indianapolis Indiana

This is one of the first appetizers I ever made. I made it for a Christmas Eve buffet I hosted many years ago. Not only was it easy, but people came back for seconds and even thirds! This can be mixed up to a day ahead of time and placed in the oven just before guests arrive.

3 cups Bisquik (or Jiffy) baking mix   *2 tablespoons cold water*

1 pound sausage (hot or mild)   *10-ounces sharp cheddar cheese, grated*

Preheat oven to 350°F. Combine raw sausage, water and cheese. Mix in Bisquik and combine well. Shape into 1-inch balls. Place on ungreased baking sheet. (For ease in cleaning I place on parchment paper on baking sheet). Bake 20 minutes. Serve immediately.

Serves 10

Smoked Beef Cheese Ball

Cindy Newsom, Walker Louisiana

Two 2 ¼-ouunce packages smoked beef   *1 tablespoon Accent*

Two 8-ounce packages cream cheese   *1 tablespoon Worcestershire sauce*

6 green onions, finely chopped

Cut smoked beef in cubes, reserving ½ cup of cubed beef to roll cheese ball in. Mix cream cheese, onions, Accent, Worcestershire sauce, smoked beef and make into ball. Wrap in wax paper or foil and put in freezer for a few minutes, then roll cheese ball in ½ cup smoked beef you had reserved. Chill completely and serve with crackers. (I use Townhouse crackers)
Serves 6 to 8

Spicy Bean Dip

Terri Grimes, Indianapolis Indiana

1 medium onion, finely chopped	*Two 15-ounce cans black beans*
2 jalapeno peppers, finely minced	*1 tablespoon minced garlic*
1 habanera pepper, finely minced	*½ teaspoon ground cumin*
1 teaspoon cumin seed	*2 tablespoons sour cream*
2 tablespoons butter	*2 cups grated sharp cheddar cheese*

Drain black beans, reserving juice from 1 can. Place the beans and the reserved juice from 1 can in a food processor or blender and puree. Sauté onion, peppers, cumin seed and garlic in the butter until the onion is done (soft) but not brown. Place these ingredients in a microwave save dish with all the remaining ingredients except the cheese. Microwave on high about 3 minutes. Stir then heat an additional 3 minutes. Remove from microwave and stir in the cheese until completely melted and blended with the other ingredients. Serve hot with tortilla chips.

Serves 6 to 8

Spinach & Artichoke Dip

Greg Grimes, Indianapolis Indiana

I make this easy, impressive appetizer every Christmas Eve for our annual open house buffet. This is one of those dishes people look forward to all year.

One 10-ounce box frozen spinach, thawed

1/4 cup butter

1 tablespoon fresh minced garlic

2 tablespoons finely minced onion

¼ cup all-purpose flour

1 pint heavy cream

¼ cup chicken broth

2 teaspoons fresh lemon juice

½ teaspoon hot sauce

½ teaspoon salt

2/3 cup grated Romano cheese

¼ cup sour cream

½ cup shredded white cheddar cheese

12-ounce jar artichoke hearts, drained, coarsely chopped

Strain spinach and squeeze through cheesecloth to remove as much liquid as possible. Mince the drained spinach and set aside. In a 2-quart saucepan over medium heat, sauté garlic and onion in butter until golden, about 3 - 5 minutes. Stir in flour and cook for 1 minute. Slowly whisk in cream and broth and continue cooking until boiling. Once boiling, stir in Romano, lemon juice, hot sauce, and salt; stir until cheese has melted; remove from heat and allow to cool for 5 minutes. Stir sour cream into pan, and then fold in dry spinach and artichoke hearts. Fold the mixture into a microwave-safe serving dish, or into several serving-size dishes. Sprinkle cheddar evenly over top(s). At this point, the dip can be refrigerated until ready to serve, if desired. Microwave dip on 50% power just until cheese has melted. Serve with tortilla chips for dipping.

Serves 6 to 8

Tuna Mold

Cindy Newsom, Walker Louisiana

In addition to serving this as an appetizer it also makes a light and refreshing luncheon dish for when the ladies stop by.

Two 6 ½-ounce cans tuna

Two packages unflavored gelatin

½ cup cold water (to dissolve gelatin)

2 cups mayonnaise

2 eggs, hard boiled

4 green onions, finely chopped

Red pepper to taste

Salt and pepper to taste

Mix gelatin with water and heat on stove until dissolved. Set aside to cool. After gelatin mixture is cool, mix with other ingredients. Pour into greased mold. Place in refrigerator to set. When set, turn mold onto serving plate. Serve with various kinds of crackers or toasted breads.
Serves 6 to 8

Zesty Cheese Straws

Terri Grimes, Indianapolis Indiana

½ (1 stick) cup butter, room temperature

1 pound shredded sharp Cheddar, room temperature

1 ½ cups all-purpose flour

1 teaspoon salt

¼ teaspoon ground red pepper

Preheat the oven to 300°F. In a mixing bowl, cream the butter until light and fluffy. Add the cheese and mix until blended. Add the flour, salt, and red pepper, and mix to form a dough. Refrigerate for 30 minutes to firm up the dough, then place it in a cookie press, fitted with a ridged tip. Pipe the dough in 2-inch strips onto a lightly greased cookie sheet. Bake for 10 to 15 minutes or until lightly browned. Remove to racks to cool.

Yield 5 dozen.

Soups

Black Bean Soup

Chicken Noodle Soup

Creamy Asparagus Soup

French Onion Soup

German Potato Soup

Ham and Lima Bean Soup

Italian Sausage Pasta Soup

Kentucky Burgoo

Lentil Soup

Lo-fat Potato Bean Soup

Navy Bean Soup

Pepperpot Soup

Senate Bean Soup

Tortilla Soup

Tortellini and Cheese Chicken Soup

Black Bean Soup

Terri Grimes, Indianapolis Indiana

1 pound black beans	*1 green pepper, chopped*
Two 15-ounce cans chicken broth	*2 ham hocks*
2 onions, chopped	*3 cloves garlic, crushed*
2-ounces salt pork, diced	*1 teaspoon cumin*
1 teaspoon paprika	*¼ teaspoon chili powder*
2 teaspoons red wine vinegar	

Soak beans overnight. Drain and put beans in stockpot, covering with water. Simmer until tender, approximately 1 hour. Drain; put all ingredients in slow cooker and cook on low for 8 hours.

Serves 6

Chicken Noodle Soup

Terri Grimes, Indianapolis Indiana

One of the most comforting dishes is good old Chicken Noodle Soup. Whether you are fighting a cold or just want a yummy lunch, this soup can't be beat!

8 cups chicken broth (home-made is best)	*Salt to taste*
	1 bay leaf
1 stalk celery, chopped	*1 cup flat egg noodles (uncooked)*
1 small onion, minced	*1 cup cooked chicken meat, cut into bite-size pieces*
2 medium carrots, peeled and sliced	
Salt and pepper to taste	*¼ cup chopped fresh parsley*

Simmer celery, onion and carrots, salt, pepper and bay leaf in chicken broth for about 20 minutes or until carrots are tender. Add the noodles, chicken and fresh parsley. Simmer until the noodles are tender, about 8 minutes. Serve.

Serves 4 to 6

Creamy Asparagus Soup

Terri Grimes, Indianapolis Indiana

2 tablespoons butter

1 leek, thinly sliced

2 tablespoons flour

2 cups chicken broth

1 pound asparagus, trimmed, chopped

2 tablespoons fresh chopped parsley

1 cup heavy cream

Salt and pepper to taste

Fresh chopped parsley for garnish, optional

In a medium saucepan, cook leeks in butter over medium-low heat until tender. Add flour and stir until well. Add chicken broth, chopped asparagus, and parsley. Bring to boil, stirring constantly. Reduce heat to low, cover, and simmer for 15 minutes, or until asparagus is tender. Carefully, working with about 1 to 2 cups at a time, blend or process until smooth; return to the saucepan and add cream. Heat through. Add salt and pepper or to taste. Garnish with fresh chopped parsley, if desired.

Serves 4

French Onion Soup

Cindy Newsom, Walker Louisiana

Make a double batch and freeze in containers for a quick appetizer or snack.

2 Sticks (1/2 pound) butter

8-10 Large Vidalia onions, sliced

Eight (15-ounce cans Campbell's Double Strength Beef Broth

8 teaspoons Worcestershire Sauce

1 teaspoon black pepper

French bread toasted or large croutons

1 pound Provolone cheese, sliced

Melt butter in large pot. Slice onions then cut slices in half. Sauté onions in butter until clear. Add in beef broth, Worcestershire sauce and pepper. Simmer approximately 4-5 hours. When ready to eat, place soup in bowl, top with bread of your choice, cover with provolone cheese and heat in microwave until cheese is melted. ENJOY!

Serves 6

German Potato Soup

Terri Grimes, Indianapolis Indiana

A comforting soup to have on a cold winter's day. I love to serve this soup with cloverleaf potato rolls. It's hearty enough to serve for dinner.

1 large onion, chopped

2 cloves garlic, minced

3 stalks celery, diced

2 tablespoons butter

3 – 4 potatoes, peeled and diced

Two 14-ounce cans chicken broth

1 ½ cups milk

1 tablespoon cornstarch

Shredded cheddar cheese for garnish

Crumbled bacon for garnish

Green onions, sliced, for garnish

In soup pot sauté onion, garlic and celery in butter until tender.   Add potatoes and chicken broth. Simmer 20 minutes or until potatoes are tender. Whisk milk and cornstarch together. Add milk mixture to soup. Simmer several minutes until milk is hot, and soup is thickened. Serve with grated cheese, crumbled bacon and green onions sprinkled on top of each bowl.

Serves 4 - 6

Ham and Lima Bean Soup

Terri Grimes, Indianapolis Indiana

1 ½ cups chopped onion

1 cup diced carrots

4 tablespoons butter

2 teaspoons garlic powder

1 teaspoon Mrs. Dash

1 tablespoon lemon juice

1 1/2 cups diced ham

10-ounces frozen baby lima beans

2 teaspoons dried marjoram

1/2 cup fresh chopped parsley

4 cups water

Salt and pepper, to taste

In a Dutch oven or heavy stockpot over medium heat, sauté onion and carrots in the butter for 6 minutes. Add garlic powder and herb seasoning, and lemon juice. Cook until onions are soft. Add ham, lima beans, marjoram, parsley, and water. Bring ham and lima bean soup to a boil; reduce heat, cover, and simmer 20 minutes, stirring occasionally. Serve ham and lima bean soup with homemade cornbread, if desired.

Serves 6 to 8.

Italian Sausage Pasta Soup

Terri Grimes, Indianapolis Indiana

When my husband and I were dating I made this soup and brought him a piping hot thermos full to his work for lunch. Every time I make this soup for him now he says it reminds him of that day and puts a smile on his face. I won't say that this soup made him fall in love with me, but it didn't hurt.

1 pound Italian sausage (hot or sweet)	*1 cup water*
One 28-ounce can diced tomatoes	*1 teaspoon basil*
One 14-ounce can chicken broth	*1 teaspoon oregano*
One 8-ounce can tomato sauce	*One 16-ounce package Green Giant® Pasta Accents (Garlic flavor)**

Roll sausage into small bite sized balls and place in soup pot. Add water to the depth of 1 inch. Cover pot and simmer 10 minutes. Drain. Add tomatoes, chicken broth, tomato sauce, water and seasonings. Simmer covered 20 minutes. Stir in frozen pasta. Simmer 5 minutes or until pasta and vegetables are done. We like to serve this soup with a tablespoon (or more) of freshly grated Parmesan cheese on top.

*Pasta Accents is pasta, broccoli, carrots and corn in a seasoned sauce and can be found in the frozen vegetable section of your grocery.

Serves 4 to 6

Kentucky Burgoo

Terri Grimes, Indianapolis Indiana

Burgoo dates back to before the civil war and is a favorite at Kentucky Derby time. Owensboro KY is the Burgoo capital. Every May they hold a BBQ festival and you see vats of Burgoo lining the streets as teams compete for bragging rights. The vats are so large that they stir the Burgoo with boat paddles.

1 pound mixed cooked meats (beef, lamb, pork, chicken, game, etc.)

1/2 gallon chicken stock

1/2 gallon beef stock

1 tablespoon Worcestershire sauce

1 cup tomatoes, diced

1 large onion, diced

1 stalk celery, diced

1 green pepper, diced

1 large potato, diced

2 large carrots, diced

1/4 cup peas

1/2 cup frozen okra, sliced

1/4 cup frozen lima beans

1/2 cup frozen yellow corn

2 teaspoons garlic, minced

Salt and pepper to taste

Combine all ingredients and bring to a boil. Reduce heat and simmer for 2 hours, skimming the top as needed.

Serves 6

Lentil Soup

Terri Grimes, Indianapolis Indiana

1 smoked ham hock	*1 large carrot, peeled and diced*
1 ½ cups dried lentils	*1 stalk celery, diced*
5 cups water	*1 teaspoon salt*
One 14-ounce can chicken broth	*½ teaspoon pepper*
One 28-ounce can diced tomatoes	*½ teaspoon parsley flakes*
1 medium onion, diced	*1 bay leaf*
2 cloves garlic, minced	*½ teaspoon thyme*

Combine all ingredients in a large soup pot. Bring to boil and immediately reduce heat to low. Simmer covered 1 hour or until lentils and vegetables are tender. Serves 4 to 6

Lo-fat Potato Bean Soup

Terri Grimes, Indianapolis Indiana

½ cup diced celery	*3 medium potatoes, peeled and cubed*
2 medium carrots, grated	*2 tablespoons dried dillweed*
1 clove garlic, minced	*One 15-ounce can Northern Beans, drained*
2 teaspoons margarine	
4 cups chicken broth	*½ cup plain nonfat yogurt*
	1 tablespoon flour

In large saucepan sauté celery, carrots and garlic in margarine. Stir in broth, potatoes and dillweed. Heat to boiling, reduce heat and simmer, covered, 15 minutes or until potatoes are tender (not mushy). With back of spoon mash about ½ of the potatoes in the broth. Add northern beans. Combine yogurt and flour. Stir into soup. Cook until thick and bubbly (1 –2 minutes).

Serves 4

Navy Bean Soup

Greg Grimes, Indianapolis Indiana

Who better to tell you how to make Navy Bean soup than the Navy! This is from a regulation cookbook given to United States Navy messmen in 1944. I dedicate this recipe in honor of my father who served in the US Navy 1939 – 1945. Although he was a Electricians mate 1st Class, one of his extra duties was as messman. I am sure Dad saw more than his share of Navy Bean Soup.

5 Pounds, 8 Ounces Beans, Navy, dried	*1 Teaspoon Cloves, whole*
Water, cold To cover	*8 Ounces Flour*
5 Gallons Ham Stock	*1 Quart Water, cold*
1 Pound Onions, chopped	*2 Teaspoons Pepper*
8 Ham Bones	*½ Cup Salt, if needed*

Pick over, wash and soak beans, in water to cover, 2 to 3 hours. Add ham stock, onions, bones and cloves. Heat to boiling temperature. Let simmer 2 to 3 hours. Remove bones. Blend together flour and water into a smooth paste. Stir into soup. Add pepper, and salt if needed. Reheat to boiling temperature.

Serves 100 (Approx. 6 Gallons)

Pepperpot Soup

Mark Danziger, Cayman Islands Caribbean

Coco is very similar to potato, so you could use potatoes if coco is not available. Serve with crusty bread for a perfect meal after a full day of scuba diving.

1 pound shin of beef, cubed	*1 fresh green chili*
8-ounces salt beef, cubed	*8-ounces yam, sliced*
1 pound callaloo, trimmed and chopped	*8-ounces coco, sliced*
2 onions, chopped finely	*8-ounces unshelled prawns (shrimp)*
2 garlic cloves, crushed	*4 ½ cups beef stock*
4 spring onion (scallions), chopped	*1 tablespoon butter*
1 teaspoon dried thyme	*4-ounces okra, trimmed and sliced*
	Salt and pepper to taste

Put beef and salt beef in a large saucepan. Cover with water and bring to a boil. Reduce heat, cover and simmer 1 ½ hours. Meanwhile, put callaloo in another saucepan, covering with cold water. Bring to a boil and cook for 10 minutes. Drain and puree in a food processor or blender. Add the callaloo puree, onion, garlic, spring onions, thyme, chili, yam, coco and prawns to the meat. Salt and pepper to taste. Add the beef stock and simmer 20 minutes or until coco and yam are soft. Melt butter in small sauté pan. Fry okra in butter until golden brown. Add okra to soup and cook an additional 5 minutes. Discard chili. Pour soup into warm soup bowls and serve.

Serves 4 to 6

Senate Bean Soup

Terri Grimes, Indianapolis Indiana

1 pound dried northern beans	*2 medium onions, chopped*
5 quarts water	*1 cup chopped celery*
2 chicken bullion cubes	*2 large cloves garlic, minced*
1 smoked ham hock	*½ teaspoon salt*
3 medium potatoes, diced	*½ teaspoon pepper*

Cover beans with water and let stand overnight. Drain liquid. Add water, broth and ham hock. Cover and simmer 2 hours, or until beans are tender. Add potatoes, onions, celery, garlic salt and pepper and simmer another hour.

Serves 4 to 6

Tortilla Soup

Terri Grimes, Indianapolis Indiana

2 boneless skinless chicken breasts, cubed	*1/8 teaspoon pepper*
	1 green Chile, seeded and chopped
1 onion, finely chopped	*2 tablespoons vegetable oil*
1 clove garlic, crushed	*4 corn tortillas, cut into 1/4 inch strips*
3 tomatoes, peeled and chopped	*½ cup shredded Monterey Jack cheese*
4 cups chicken broth	*2 tablespoons chopped fresh cilantro*
1/4 teaspoon salt	

Combine chicken breasts, onion, garlic, tomatoes, broth, salt, pepper and green Chile in slow cooker. Cover and cook on low 7-8 hours. Heat oil in large skillet and add tortilla strips. Cook, stirring, over medium heat until crisp; drain on paper towels. Put a tablespoon of Monterey Jack cheese in each bowl. Ladle tortilla soup on top. Sprinkle with tortilla strips and chopped cilantro.

Serves 4

Tortellini and Cheese Chicken Soup

Terri Grimes, Indianapolis Indiana

4 1/2 quarts chicken broth

One 8-ounce package fresh cheese-filled tortellini

3/4 pound spinach leaves, stems removed

1 pound boneless, skinless chicken breasts, cut in 1/2-inch pieces

8-ounces mushrooms, sliced

1 medium red bell pepper, chopped

1 cup cooked rice

1 ½ teaspoons dried basil

Grated Parmesan cheese

Rinse, drain and chop spinach leaves. In an 8 to 10-quart kettle or Dutch oven, bring the chicken broth to a boil over high heat. Add tortellini, and cook for about 4 minutes, just until tender. Add spinach, chicken, mushrooms, bell pepper, rice, and basil, then return to a boil over high heat. Reduce heat, cover and simmer for about 3 minutes, or until chicken is no longer pink in the center. Ladle into bowls. Sprinkle each serving with Parmesan cheese to taste and serve.

Serves 6

Salads

Carrot Salad

Coleslaw

Fandango Salad

Greek Salad

Hollywood Brown Derby Cobb Salad

Jello Salad

Krabby Salad

Lime Jello Salad

Macaroni Salad

Orange Pineapple Salad

Overnight Lettuce

Potato Salad

Ramen Slaw

Spring Salad

Waldorf Salad

Watergate Salad

Carrot Salad

Terri Grimes, Indianapolis Indiana

Kids are so thrilled that you are letting them eat jello at dinner that they don't realize they are eating a veggie. Sneaky, very sneaky!

One 3-ounce package orange jello	*1 cup boiling water*
2 large carrots, finely grated	*¼ cup cold water*
One 8-ounce can crushed pineapple	

Dissolve jello in boiling water. Mix in grated carrot, crushed pineapple (do not drain pineapple) and cold water. Refrigerate until jello is set, approximately 2 to 3 hours.

Serves 4

Coleslaw

Terri Grimes, Indianapolis Indiana

We serve this sweet, creamy coleslaw with pulled pork sandwiches. It provides a perfect contrast to the smoky meat and tangy BBQ sauce.

1 head cabbage, finely shredded	*½ cup sugar*
2 large carrots, finely grated	*1 teaspoon salt*
2 Tablespoon mayonnaise	*1/8 teaspoon black pepper*
1 cup half and half	*6 Tablespoons apple cider vinegar*

Place grated cabbage and carrots into a large bowl. Set aside. In lidded jar mix all ingredients except cabbage and carrots. Shake several minutes to mix well. Pour dressing over cabbage and carrots. Toss to mix well. Refrigerate slaw 1 hour before serving.

Serves 6 to 8

Fandango Salad

Terri Grimes, Indianapolis Indiana

Sometimes I substitute a can of mandarin oranges for the apple. If I really want to impress I use both. Everyone loves this salad!

4 cups mixed salad greens (or 1 bag Spring Mix greens)

1 Granny Smith apple, chopped into bite sized pieces

½ cup chopped pecans (or walnuts)

½ cup seedless raspberry jam

¼ cup red wine vinegar

2 tablespoons oil

1/3 cup crumbed blue cheese

In small bowl whisk raspberry jam, vinegar and oil until well combined. Set aside. In salad bowl combine salad greens, chopped apple and pecans. Toss salad with dressing. Sprinkle blue cheese on salad and lightly toss. Serve.

Serves 4 to 6

Greek Salad

Terri Grimes, Indianapolis Indiana

1 tablespoon balsamic vinegar

1 tablespoon sugar

1 English Cucumber, peeled and sliced

1 small red onion, thinly sliced

1 cup cherry tomatoes, cut in halves

½ cup calamata or black olives

2 tablespoon lemon juice

1 tablespoon Olive oil

½ teaspoon Kosher salt

1/8 teaspoon black pepper

2 tablespoons fresh basil, chopped

1/3 cup Feta cheese, crumbled

In medium bowl mix balsamic vinegar and sugar together. Toss in cucumber slices, red onion slices, tomatoes and black olives. Drizzle lemon juice and olive oil onto vegetables. Toss to coat. Sprinkle with seasonings. Add basil and feta cheese. Toss lightly and serve. This salad does not store well overnight.

Serves 4 to 6

Hollywood Brown Derby Cobb Salad

Kate Chaplin, Indianapolis Indiana

When I lived in LA, while going to film school this was one of my favorite places to eat and definitely my favorite dish.

Salad:

½ head iceberg lettuce

½ bunch watercress lettuce

1 small bunch chicory lettuce

½ head romaine lettuce

2 medium tomatoes

½ breast turkey, poached

1 avocado

6 strips of bacon

3 eggs, hard cooked

½ cup Hollywood Brown Derby's French dressing

2 tablespoons chives, chopped

½ cup bleu cheese, crumbled

Brown Derby French Dressing:

1 cup water

1 teaspoon sugar

2 ½ tablespoons salt

1 tablespoon Worcestershire sauce

1 clove garlic, chopped

1 cup red wine vinegar

Juice of ½ a lemon

1 tablespoon ground black pepper

1 teaspoon English mustard

1 cup of olive oil

3 cups salad oil

Finely chop all greens and add to salad bowl. Finely dice tomatoes, turkey, avocado, bacon, and eggs. Add to salad greens. Make dressing by blending together all ingredients except oils, then add olive and salad oils, and mix well again. Blend well before mixing with salad. Toss salad with dressing. Sprinkle bleu cheese and chives on salad, toss lightly and serve.

Yield 48-ounces salad dressing (Keep refrigerated)

Salad serves 4 to 6

Jello Salad

Cindy Newsom, Walker Louisiana

One 3-ounce package Lemon Jell-o

One-half 3-ounce package Lime Jell-o

1 Cup Boiling water

One 8-ounce can crushed pineapple

¾ cup evaporated milk

¼ cup Mayonnaise

8-ounces cottage cheese

¼ teaspoon Salt

½ cup Nuts (your choice)

Empty Jell-O's in large bowl, add hot water mix well. Let cool 15 – 20 minutes till chilled but not set. Add remaining ingredients stir well. Pour into mold or bowl and refrigerate 4 hours or until set. Dip mold into hot water for a few seconds and turn onto serving plate.

Serves 4 to 6

Krabby Salad

Debra A. Kemp, Carmel Indiana

As a busy author working on the third book in my Pendragon Series, (Book One; The Firebrand, Book Two; The Recruit) this salad makes a nice lunch or light supper. I keep it in the fridge to nibble on for those days that I can't tear myself away from my writing. This salad keeps writers from getting 'krabby'.

One 8-ounce package Rotini pasta

One 8-ounce package imitation crab (flake style)

One 8-ounce package frozen peas, thawed

Diced onion to taste

Diced bell pepper to taste

½ cup mayonnaise

¼ cup Italian dressing

Salt and pepper to taste

Garlic salt to taste

Cook pasta al dente and drain. Combine the mayonnaise and Italian dressing until smooth. In a large bowl, mix everything together. Allow to chill. Great as a side dish or main dish.

Serves 4

Lime Jello Salad

Terri Grimes, Indianapolis Indiana

My sister in law had the idea of using orange jello instead of lime. That made this taste like a yummy orange dream sickle. Both ways are refreshing and delicious.

One 3-ounce package lime jello   *One 8-ounce package cream cheese*

1 cup boiling water   *1 cup miniature marshmallows*

One 8-ounce can crushed pineapple   *8-ounces cool whip, thawed*

Add pkg of jello to boiling water. Stir to dissolve. Leave on medium heat while adding pineapple (do not drain). Add cream cheese, continuing to stir over medium heat. Add marshmallows and stir to dissolve. Pour jello mixture into a bowl and refrigerate 15-20 minutes to cool. Fold thawed cool whip into cooled mixture. Place in jello mold and refrigerate 3 hours or until set.

Serves 6

Macaroni Salad

Terri Grimes, Indianapolis Indiana

A picnic wouldn't complete without homemade macaroni salad. Light yet filling and oh so yummy, this recipe is a summer time staple in our house.

4 cups cooked macaroni

1 cup sliced celery

1/2 cup sliced scallions

1 small green pepper, chopped

¼ cup chopped red pepper

2 tablespoons finely chopped parsley

1 cup mayonnaise

2 tablespoons vinegar

½ teaspoon ground pepper

1 teaspoon salt

Combine macaroni, celery, scallions, green pepper, red pepper and parsley in a large bowl; toss to mix. In a small bowl, mix the mayonnaise and vinegar together until smooth. Add to the macaroni mixture. Add pepper and salt to taste and mix well. Refrigerate several hours before serving, adding more mayonnaise if needed.

Serves 6

Orange Pineapple Salad

Terri Grimes, Indianapolis Indiana

This is a great Jello salad that little ones can help make. This was the first of many dishes Jasmine, my granddaughter, helped me make.

One 6-ounce can mandarin oranges

One 8-ounce can pineapple chunks

One 3-ounce package orange jello

8-ounces cool whip, thawed

Drain oranges and pineapple chunks. Put oranges and pineapple in bowl. Sprinkle dry jello over fruits and mix until jello is combined. Fold in cool whip. Refrigerate 2 hours or more.

Serves 4

Overnight Lettuce

Terri Grimes, Indianapolis Indiana

One of my daughter's favorite dishes when she was growing up. You need to make this one the night before you serve it. And if my daughter Brooke is in your house put a lock on the fridge because she will poke her fingers in this dish the night you make it, getting little sample tastes.

1 head iceberg lettuce, chopped	*1 cup mayonnaise*
2 hard boiled eggs, chopped	*1 tablespoon sugar*
1 cup frozen peas, thawed	*1 cup grated cheddar cheese*
½ lb bacon, fried and crumbled	*2 tomatoes, chopped*

In 2 quart casserole dish layer lettuce, eggs, peas and bacon in that order. Mix mayonnaise and sugar. Spread mayonnaise mixture over dish. Top with cheddar cheese. Sprinkle chopped tomatoes over top entire dish. Refrigerate overnight or at least 8 hours.

Serves 4 to 6

Potato Salad

Terri Grimes, Indianapolis Indiana

Out of all of the countless versions of potato salad I've concocted, this version is actually pretty darned good.

2 pounds potatoes, peeled and chopped	½ cup mayonnaise
½ teaspoon salt	1 tablespoon yellow mustard
1/8 teaspoon pepper	2 teaspoons cider vinegar
½ teaspoon basil	salt and pepper to taste
½ teaspoon oregano	2 teaspoons sugar
½ teaspoon garlic salt	1 tablespoon chopped sweet pickle
1 teaspoon butter	

Put potatoes in saucepan with enough water to cover. Add salt, pepper, basil, oregano, garlic salt and butter. Simmer until potatoes are done, but not mushy. (Approximately 15 minutes) Drain potatoes. In separate bowl combine mayonnaise, mustard, vinegar, sugar, sweet pickle and salt and pepper to taste. Toss potatoes with mayonnaise mixture and refrigerate until chilled.

Ramen Slaw

Terri Grimes, Indianapolis Indiana

Trust me when I say that after you taste this you'll make it again and again.

One 10-ounce bag slaw mix

4 green onion, chopped

2 tablespoons sesame seeds

2-ounces slivered almonds

1package chicken flavored ramen noodles, reserve flavor packet

1 tablespoons butter

2/3 cup oil

2 tablespoons rice vinegar

4 tablespoons sugar

½ teaspoon pepper

2 tablespoons soy sauce

Sauté almonds and sesame seeds in butter until golden. Be careful as they burn quickly. Set aside. In bowl place slaw, green onions and crushed ramen noodles in layers. Place sesame seeds and almonds on top. In small bowl mix oil, vinegar, sugar, pepper, soy sauce and reserved flavor packet from the pkg of ramen noodles. Whisk until well combined. Pour dressing on slaw and toss. Do not do that until you are ready to serve. Serve immediately after tossing.

Serves 4 to 6

Spring Salad

Terri Grimes, Indianapolis Indiana

4 cups mixed salad greens or 1 bag
Spring Mix greens

¼ cup thinly sliced red onion

¼ cup pine nuts

¼ cup Gorgonzola cheese, crumbled

2 tablespoons balsamic vinegar

2 tablespoons sugar

2 tablespoons extra virgin olive oil

Toast pine nuts in a dry non-stick skillet until golden. Set aside. In bowl whisk vinegar, sugar and oil until well combined. In salad bowl combine greens, onions and toasted pine nuts. Toss with dressing. Top with cheese and serve.

Serves 4 to 6

Waldorf Salad

Terri Grimes, Indianapolis Indiana

First served at the famous Waldorf-Astoria Hotel in Manhattan, my recipe is slightly sweeter. I prefer using two types of apple in my Waldorf Salad. I choose apples of different color, like Granny Smith and McIntosh to add flavor.

¼ cup mayonnaise

¼ cup plain yogurt

2 teaspoons sugar

2 teaspoons lemon juice

2 apples

2 celery stalks

½ cup chopped walnuts

In small salad bowl, combine mayonnaise, yogurt and lemon juice, to taste. Core apples, cut into bite size pieces, dice celery. Add both to salad bowl, fold in nuts. Chill up to two hours. Toss before serving.

Serves 4

Watergate Salad

Terri Grimes, Indianapolis Indiana

One 3.4-ounce package Instant Pistachio Pudding

8- ounces Cool Whip, thawed

2 Cups Miniature marshmallows

One 15-ounce can crushed pineapple

½ cup chopped Pecans (optional)

Pour pineapple into mixing bowl, do not drain. Sprinkle dry pudding mix over crushed pineapple and stir well. Mix in pecans and marshmallows into pineapple mixture and combine well. Fold in cool whip. Refrigerate 2 hours or until firm. Serve cold.

Serves 4 to 6

Main Dishes

BEEF

America's Favorite Pot Roast

BBQ Beef Sandwiches

Beef Bourguignon

Bloody Mary Meat Loaf

Brisket and Seasonings

Burgers on the Grill

Cowboy Stew

French Pot Roast

Goulash

Lazy Pigs in a Blanket

Meatloaf

Prize Winning Chili

Stuffed Peppers

CHICKEN

Beer Can Chicken

Better N Chicken & Dumplings

Bourbon Street Chicken

California Thai linguini

Cheaters Chicken Cacciatore

Cheesy Crockpot Chicken

Chick Rolls

Chicken and Sun-Dried Tomatoes Fettuccini

Chicken Enchiladas

Chicken Fajitas

Chicken Piccata

Chicken Stirfry

Chicken with Lemon and Green Onion Sauce

Crunchy Tenders

Easy Chicken Marinade

Lemon Garlic Chicken

Naked Chef Chicken

Sesame Sweet Chicken

Steamed Cornish Hens

Szechwan Chicken

PORK

Baby Back Ribs

Bowtie Pasta with Basil Cream Sauce

Broccoli & Ham Quiche

Easy BBQ Pork Sandwich

Grilled Ham Steak

Red Beans and Rice

SEAFOOD

Crab Cakes

Crawfish Etouffee'

Salmon Steaks

Scalloped Oysters

Shrimp Skewers with Fruit Salsa

America's Favorite Pot Roast

Julie Cameron, Des Moines Iowa

Hard to believe, since this is such a full flavored dish, but this is a Weight Watchers recipe. If you are following Weight Watchers point system a heaping serving of this dish is only 7 points.

3 ½ pounds sirloin tip roast, trimmed	*2 small onions, sliced*
¼ cup flour	*1 stalk celery, cut in 2-inch pieces*
2 teaspoons salt	*One 2-ounce Jar mushrooms, drained*
1/8 teaspoon pepper	*3 tablespoons flour*
3 carrots, peeled and sliced	*¼ cup water*
3 potatoes, peeled and quartered	

Trim all excess fat from roast; brown and drain if using chuck or another highly marbled cut. Combine 1/4 cup flour, the salt and pepper. Coat meat with the flour mixture. Place all vegetables except mushrooms in Crock-Pot and top with roast (cut roast in half, if necessary, to fit easily). Spread mushrooms evenly over top of roast. Cover and cook on Low for 10 to 12 hours. If desired, turn to High during last hour to soften vegetables and make a gravy. To thicken gravy, make a smooth paste of the 3 tablespoons flour and the water and stir into Crock-Pot. Season to taste.

Serves 4 to 6

BBQ Beef Sandwiches

Julie Cameron, Des Moines Iowa

Since you use a slow cooker this is a super simple recipe. And at only 7.5 Weight Watcher points you don't have any excuse not to try this recipe.

2 ½ pounds lean boneless chuck roast

¼ cup tomato ketchup

1 tablespoon Dijon-style mustard

2 tablespoons brown sugar

1 garlic clove, crushed

1 tablespoon Worcestershire sauce

2 tablespoons red wine vinegar

¼ teaspoon liquid smoke flavoring

¼ teaspoon salt

1/8 teaspoon pepper

10 French rolls or sandwich buns

Place beef in slow cooker. Combine remaining ingredients, except rolls. Pour over meat. Cover and cook on LOW 8 to 9 hours. Refrigerate or prepare sandwiches now. Shred beef by pulling it apart with 2 forks. Add one cup sauce. Reheat mixture in microwave or on stovetop. Spoon on warm, open-face rolls or buns. Top with additional warm sauce if desired.

Serves 10

Beef Bourguignon

Terri Grimes, Indianapolis Indiana

This is France's version of Beef Stew. After tasting this you'll never go back to plain old beef stew again. This is so easy to make and the results are phenomenal! The rule of thumb on cooking with wine is to use a wine that you would drink. I like to use a cabernet sauvignon with this recipe.

4 slices thick bacon, cubed	*2 tablespoons tomato paste*
1 pound beef cubes	*1 tablespoon fresh thyme*
3 medium carrots, peeled and sliced	*1 teaspoon kosher salt*
1 medium onion, diced	*½ teaspoon black pepper*
2 cloves garlic, minced	*1 bay leaf*
2 shallots, finely minced	*6 tablespoons butter*
2 tablespoons olive oil	*18 pearl onions*
2 ½ cups beef broth	*One 8-ounce mushrooms*
2 cups dry red wine	*2 tablespoons all purpose flour*

Sauté bacon in deep pan. Discard drippings except for 2 tablespoons. Set bacon aside, leaving reserved drippings in pan. Sauté beef cubes in reserved bacon drippings. Remove beef. Sauté carrots, diced onions, garlic, and shallots in olive oil approximately 5 minutes. Return bacon and beef to pan. Add beef broth, wine, tomato paste and herbs. Cover and simmer 1 ½ hours or more. Peel onions and place in saucepan. Cover with just enough water to cover. Bring water to boil and boil onions for 3 minutes. Drain and dry onions on paper towels. Sauté pearl onions in 2 tablespoons butter 5 minutes or until lightly golden. Put onions into beef mixture. Cut mushrooms in half. Sauté in 2 tablespoons butter 3 – 5 minutes. Add mushrooms to beef mixture. Mix 2 tablespoons cornstarch and 2 tablespoons soft butter. Stir into beef mixture, stirring constantly and simmer till thickened. Serve with crusty bread and wine.

Serves 6

Bloody Mary Meat Loaf

Bonita DelRey, Chicago Illinois

A bonus of this recipe is you get two loaves for the work of one. If ground veal is difficult to find, ground turkey makes a suitable substitute.

1 ½ lbs ground veal	4 bay leaves, roughly crumbled
1 ½ lbs ground pork	2 tablespoons thyme, crumbled
1 ½ lbs ground beef	½ cup chopped parsley
1 cup dry bread crumbs	2 minced onions
3 eggs	½ teaspoon salt
½ cup ketchup	1/8 teaspoon pepper
1 ½ cup liquid Bloody Mary mix	4 to 6 bacon strips, uncooked

Preheat oven to 325°F. In medium bowl mix all ingredients except bacon. Form into loaves and place mixture in loaf pans. (Freeze one if desired.) Top with bacon strips. Bake for 1 ¼ hours. Cool slightly before slicing.

Each Loaf Serves 8

Brisket and Seasonings

Cindy Newsom, Walker Louisiana

½ cup chili powder	1 cup salt
5 tablespoons Accent (meat tenderizer)	3 tablespoons black pepper
2 tablespoons garlic powder	1 can Coca-Cola
	10 pounds Beef Brisket, Whole

Preheat oven to 400°F. Mix spices together. (Makes enough seasoning to cook 4-5 ten-pound briskets.) Rub brisket with seasoning. Line pan with heavy duty foil. (Cut foil long enough to fold over). Place brisket in pan. Pour Coke in pan. Fold aluminum foil tight at the top and sides. Bake three hours.

Serves 6 to 8

Burgers on the Grill

Cindy Newsom, Walker Louisiana

This is one of my recipes I am always asked for.

3 pounds ground chuck	*1 tablespoon onion powder*
3 tablespoons A-1 Sauce	*1 tablespoon Season All*
3 tablespoons Worcestershire Sauce	*BBQ Sauce (I use Cattleman's)*
1 tablespoon garlic powder	*¼ Cup Water*

In large bowl mix all ingredients together. Form into patties. This will make approximately 10 to 12 large patties. Place on hot grill and cook approximately 5 minutes per side for well done or less per side if you prefer a rare burger. After cooking a few minutes, coat with BBQ Sauce, cook for a few more minutes until BBQ sauce is charred and caramelized.

Serves 10

Cowboy Stew

Julie Cameron, Des Moines Iowa

Only 7 weight Watcher points. Easy, tasty and fits into your weight watcher plan. What more could you need? This is a great dinner to come home to.

1 1/4 pounds beef stew meat	*1 teaspoon salt*
4 potatoes, unpeeled, cut into 4-inch pieces	*1/4 teaspoon pepper*
1/2 cup chopped onion	*One 28-ounce can Baked Beans in BBQ Sauce*

Mix beef, potatoes, onion, salt and pepper in 3 1/2 qt. to 4 qt. slow cooker. Spread beans over beef mixture. Cover and cook on LOW 8-10 hrs. or until beef is tender.

Serves 6

French Pot Roast

United States Navy, USA

From a regulation cookbook given to United States Navy messmen in 1944.

40 pounds boneless beef	*3 pounds flour*
2 pounds onions, finely chopped	*½ gallon tomato catsup*
¾ cup Salt	*Beef stock as needed*
3½ teaspoons pepper	*15 pounds white Potatoes*

Cut meat into 3-inch cubes. Combine meat, onion, salt and pepper. Cook in slow oven (300° F.) 20 to 30 minutes. Stir in flour. Cook until brown. Stir in tomato catsup. Add enough stock to cover the roasts. Reduce heat to 200° F. to 250° F. Cook until meat is tender. Cut potatoes French style. Add to roast 40 minutes before end of cooking period. NOTE: Use less tender cuts of meat.

Serves 100

Goulash

Jasmine Timmons, Indianapolis Indiana

My Grandma Terri asked me what my favorite dish to cook is and this is it. If you have a kid in the house make them stir it because kids like to do that.

1 pound ground beef	*Vinegar sauce*
2 cans tomatoes	*Macaroni, the curled up kind*
2 can tomato sauce	

Take meat and put it in a pan. Cut it up with a spoon in the pan and let it cook. Then put in tomatoes in a can, and more tomatoes in a can. Then you put in tomato sauce and then more tomato sauce. Then you add vinegar sauce. You can stir it if you want to. If you have a kid in the house they can stir it for you if you want it stirred. Then put macaroni in the pan. Make sure it is the curled up kind. Then let it cook and that's it. You just made goulash!

Lazy Pigs in a Blanket

Terri Grimes, Indianapolis Indiana

This is my rendition of stuffed cabbage rolls, without the hassle of rolling cabbage bundles. I created this recipe in the late 80's. I mistakenly thought cabbage rolls were titled "Pigs in a blanket" so gave the recipe the title of "Lazy Pigs in a Blanket". I didn't discover my error until years later and by then it was too late, the name had stuck.

One 14-ounce can Tomato soup

One 6-ounce can tomato sauce

1 tablespoon apple cider vinegar

¼ cup chopped onion

¼ cup chopped green pepper

¼ cup chopped celery

1 tablespoon butter

1 pound hamburger

¼ teaspoon black pepper

½ teaspoon kosher salt

2 cups shredded cabbage

2 cups sliced raw potatoes

Preheat oven to 350°F. Combine tomato soup, tomato sauce and vinegar. Set aside. Sauté onion, green pepper and celery in butter 5 minutes or until vegetables are browned. Set aside. Brown hamburger and drain. Combine browned hamburger with 13x9 baking dish layer 1 cup cabbage, 1 cup potato slices, hamburger mixture and half of the soup mixture, in that order. Layer with remaining cup of potatoes, remaining cabbage and remaining soup mixture. Cover and bake 1 hour. Remove cover and bake 20 additional minutes.

Serves 4 to 6

Meatloaf

Terri Grimes, Indianapolis Indiana

In my quest for the almighty meatloaf I found that simple is best. I tried about fifty different meatloaf recipes, and ended up takes the best parts of each and making my own recipe for the ultimate meatloaf. I serve this meatloaf with Decadent Macaroni and Cheese and a simple tossed salad. If this recipe doesn't immediately transport you back to the 50's nothing will.

1 pound ground turkey	*½ cup onion, minced finely*
1 pound ground sirloin	*½ cup green pepper, minced*
½ pound ground veal	*½ tsp pepper*
1 egg, beaten	*½ tsp kosher salt*
½ cup Panko bread crumbs	*1 tablespoon Worcestershire sauce*
1/3 cup whole milk	*One 8-ounce can tomato sauce*

Preheat oven to 350°F. Soak the Panko crumbs in the milk. Add meats to large mixing bowl. Add 4 ounces of the tomato sauce (1/2 can). Top meat mixture with rest the ingredients including milk soaked Panko crumbs. Mix by hand until everything is incorporated. Place meat mixture in a baking dish and form into a loaf. I use a 10x9 baking dish but you can use a loaf pan, round pan, 13x9 pan, or whatever pan you wish. Take remaining tomato sauce and spread evenly on top of meatloaf. Bake 1 ½ hours. Allow meatloaf to rest at least 20 minutes before slicing.

Serves 4 to 6

Prize Winning Chili

Greg Grimes, Indianapolis Indiana

I entered this chili in a chili cookoff and won People's choice with it! I was hoping to have some left over to take home for a snack but everyone consumed every last drop of this delectable chili.

1 pound lean ground beef	*2 tablespoons chili powder*
1 medium onion, chopped	*½ teaspoon garlic powder*
1 medium green pepper, chopped	*½ teaspoon onion powder*
2 cloves garlic, minced	*1 teaspoon cumin*
1 jalapeno, minced	*½ teaspoon nutmeg*
1 mild banana pepper, chopped	*½ teaspoon cinnamon*
One 28-ounce can crushed tomatoes	*2 tablespoons sugar*
One 15-ounce can tomato sauce	*1 teaspoon kosher salt*
One 15-ounce can kidney beans	*½ teaspoon black pepper*
One 15-ounce can pinto beans	*½ teaspoon red pepper flakes*
1-ounce dark chocolate, grated	*1/8 teaspoon cayenne pepper*

Brown ground beef in stockpot, draining grease. Add onion, green pepper, garlic, jalapeno and banana pepper sautéing with ground beef until vegetables are soft, approximately 5 minutes. Add tomatoes and beans, stirring to combine. Bring to just a boil and immediately turn down to a simmer. In a small bowl combine all seasonings, stirring to mix. Add seasoning blend to chili and stir well to combine. Simmer uncovered 1 ½ hours. Enjoy!

Serves 8

Stuffed Peppers

Terri Grimes, Indianapolis Indiana

6 Assorted peppers (red, yellow, green, orange)

3 vine ripened tomatoes

1 pound ground beef

1 medium onion, chopped

2 cloves garlic, minced

1 teaspoon kosher salt

½ teaspoon pepper

1 teaspoon Italian seasoning

1 teaspoon dried basil

1 teaspoon dried oregano

One 8-ounce can tomato sauce

1 cup water

¾ cup minute rice (or other instant rice)

Preheat oven to 350°F. Prepare peppers by cutting off tops and scooping out seeds. Reserve extra pepper on top that you just cut off and chop it up. Cut tops off tomatoes and scoop out guts, placing them in a small bowl to use later. Sauté ground beef, chopped peppers (from the tops you cut off), onion and garlic until beef is no longer pink and onion is translucent. Add tomato sauce, water and reserved tomato guts. (That's a technical term). Add all seasonings and simmer five minutes or until mixture is hot and bubbly. Add minute rice, cover and simmer on lowest setting 5 to 8 minutes or until rice is tender. Put scooped out peppers and tomatoes in a 13 x 9 baking dish. Bake uncovered 45 minutes.

Serves 4 to 6

Beer Can Chicken

Greg Grimes, Indianapolis Indiana

This makes the moistest, most flavorful chicken you will ever put in your mouth. Caution: Before you take the chicken to the grill, stand it up on a sheet pan, to make sure it is stable, and won't fall over when you place it on the grill.

2 tablespoons black pepper	*1 tablespoon chili powder*
3 tablespoons brown sugar	*2 tablespoons salt*
2-3 tablespoons paprika	*1 whole roasting chicken*
1 tablespoon ground cumin	*One 12-ounce can of beer*

Prepare your grill for indirect, medium-high heat grilling. Combine the first five ingredients, and rub the mixture all over the chicken. Pour out (or drink!) half the can of beer. Cut the top off the can of beer with a can opener. Stand the chicken upright, with the cavity facing down. Place the half-filled beer can in the cavity, and arrange the chicken so that it can stand up, using the two legs to form a tripod. Place the chicken, standing up, on the grill, away from the direct heat. Rotate the chicken every 15-20 minutes so it will evenly brown. The chicken will take 1 ¼ to 1 ½ hours to cook. It will be done when a thermometer, reading 175°, is inserted between the leg and the thigh.

Serves 4

Better N Chicken & Dumplings

Tammy Flowers, Hammond, Louisiana

1 chicken, cooked, de-boned and cut into bite-sized pieces

One 10-ounce can cream of chicken soup

½ cup (1 stick) melted butter

2 cups chicken broth

1 cup milk

1 cup self-rising flour

Salt and pepper to taste

Preheat oven to 350°F. Layer chicken in bottom of casserole dish. Pour melted butter over chicken. Mix flour with milk and pour over chicken. Mix soup with broth and pour over top and gently stir across top to smooth out. Bake for 45 minutes.

Serves 4

Bourbon Street Chicken

Cindy Newsom, Walker Louisiana

4 boneless, skinless chicken breasts

1 teaspoon ginger

¼ cup soy sauce

2 tablespoons dried minced onion

½ cup brown sugar, packed

¼ cup bourbon (to taste)

½ teaspoon garlic powder

Preheat oven to 375°F. Place chicken breasts in a 9x13" baking dish. Combine the ginger, soy sauce, onion flakes, sugar, bourbon and garlic powder and pour over chicken. Cover dish and place in refrigerator overnight. In a covered dish, bake in preheated oven, basting frequently, for 1 hour or until chicken is well browned and juices run clear. Also good on the grill!

Serves 4

California Thai Linguini

Terri Grimes, Indianapolis Indiana

I created this recipe inspired by a dish I experienced in Fresno California on a business trip in 2003. I find that if I set out all the ingredients on the counter before cooking I can breeze right through making this dish in no time.

1 pound linguine

4 boneless skinless chicken breasts

1 tablespoon oil

3/4 cup carrots, julienned

3/4 cup zucchini, julienned

1 cup broccoli florets

4 tablespoons fresh ginger, minced

6 tablespoons orange juice

2 tablespoons soy sauce

4 1/2 tablespoons sesame oil

3 tablespoons brown sugar

2 tablespoons rice wine vinegar

1/4 cup peanut butter

1 jalapeno, seeded and minced, (optional)

1/2 cup white wine

½ cup chopped cilantro

½ cup toasted peanuts

Cook linguini as directed on package to al dente. While linguini is cooking, grill or sauté chicken until done; slice thinly and set aside. Make peanut sauce by combining ginger, orange juice, soy sauce, sesame oil, brown sugar, vinegar and peanut butter. Mix well. Set aside. Heat wok or large skillet over medium high heat. Add oil. When oil is hot, add veggies and sauce 1 minute. Add in chicken, peanut sauce and wine, and cook until reduced by half. Place drained linguini in a large bowl. Pour sauce over, toss. Garnish with cilantro and peanuts.

Serves 4

Cheaters Chicken Cacciatore

Julie Cameron, Des Moines Iowa

Just 5.5 points on the Weight Watchers system.

6 skinless, boneless chicken breast halves

One 28-ounce jar spaghetti sauce

2 green bell peppers, seeded and cubed

8-ounces fresh mushrooms, sliced

1 onion, finely diced

2 tablespoons minced garlic

Put the chicken in the slow cooker. Top with the spaghetti sauce, green bell peppers, mushrooms, onion and garlic. Cook on low for 7 to 9 hours. Serve!

Serves 6

Cheesy Crockpot Chicken

Julie Cameron, Des Moines Iowa

This recipe is only 7.5 Weight Watcher points and that includes rice! Put it in the crockpot in the morning and when you get home from work enjoy a delicious home cooked meal that not only tastes great but is guilt free too!

2 pounds boneless skinless chicken breasts

Two 10-ounce cans 98% fat-free cream of chicken soup

One 10-ounce can cheddar cheese soup

1/4 teaspoon garlic powder

Cut chicken into bite size pieces. Put chicken in the bottom of the crockpot. Add rest of ingredients on top. Cook 8 hours on low. Serve over rice or noodles.

Serves 6 to 8

Chick Rolls

Terri Grimes, Indianapolis Indiana

These have been served at my house from anything to an appetizer to the entrée at a ladies luncheon to dinner with the family. They are one of our family favorites. I like to serve them with sweet and sour sauce for dipping.

1 pound boneless, skinless chicken breasts

One 8-ounce package Crescent rolls

2 tablespoons flour

One 2.8-ounce can Durkee fried onions

2 eggs, beaten

2 tablespoons sesame seeds

Preheat oven to 350°F. Cut chicken breasts into 1-inch pieces. In small bowl combine fried onions and flour. Take a drinking glass (or other implement) and finely crush fried onions. Remove crescent dough from packages. Separate into triangles. Cut each triangle in half. Dip raw chicken chunks in beaten egg, then roll in onion/flour mixture. Immediately place chicken chunk in the center of a triangle dough half. Pinch the edges of the dough around the chicken chunk, sealing. Place rolls on ungreased cookie sheet. Lightly brush tops of chick rolls with remaining beaten egg and sprinkle sesame seeds on top. Bake 20 minutes or until golden brown. Note: Dough handles best when it is chilled.

Yield 16 Chick rolls

Chicken and Sun-Dried Tomatoes Fettuccini

Terri Grimes, Indianapolis Indiana

This is a great summer time dish because you aren't turning your oven on. This meal goes from pantry to table is less than 30 minutes. Those are the kind of summer time dishes my family thrives on!

1/4 cup sun-dried tomatoes

1/2 cup boiling water

2 boned, skinned chicken breast halves

Salt and pepper, to taste

2 tablespoon olive oil, divided

1 medium onion, chopped

2 cups sliced mushrooms

1 clove garlic, minced

1 tablespoon chopped fresh basil

1 cup sour cream

1/2 cup grated Parmesan cheese

8-ounces Fettuccini, prepared as directed on pkg

1 tablespoon minced fresh basil

Rehydrate tomatoes in boiling water for 10 minutes; drain, reserving liquid; set aside. Season chicken with salt and pepper on both sides. Brown chicken in 1 tablespoon oil for 6 minutes on each side; set aside. Sauté onions in remaining oil until tender. Add mushrooms, garlic, basil, and tomatoes and sauté for an additional 3 minutes. Stir in sour cream and Parmesan, then slowly stir in enough reserved tomato water until desired consistency is reached. Stir in cooked fettuccini. Serve chicken breast over a bed of the pasta and garnish with basil.

Serves 2

Chicken Enchiladas

Terri Grimes, Indianapolis Indiana

If you can't find canned tomatillas merely use a green enchilada sauce instead of making your own sauce. If you can find them though, this sauce is better than any enchilada sauce out there. Well worth the extra time to make it!

3 cups water

¼ teaspoon salt

8 peppercorns

1 medium onion, quartered

1 bay leaf

1 teaspoon butter

¼ cup minced onion

1 pound boneless skinless chicken breasts

1 cup grated cheese (I use a mix of Colby and Monterey jack)

12 corn tortillas

¼ cup chopped green onion

Sauce:

2/3 cup milk

¼ cup chopped cilantro

1 egg, beaten

½ teaspoon salt

One 11-ounce can tomatillas, drained

One 4.5-ounce can chopped green chilies

Place water, chicken, peppercorns, salt, bay leaf and quartered onion into Dutch oven or 2 quart saucepan with lid. Simmer covered 45 minutes. Cool and shred chicken. Sauté minced onion in butter. Add to shredded chicken. Add ½ cup cheese to chicken mixture. Prepare the sauce by putting all sauce ingredients into a food processor or blender and processing until smooth. Spoon ¼ cup filling into each warm tortilla and roll. Place in 11x7 baking dish. Repeat until all tortillas are rolled. Pour sauce over enchiladas. Cover casserole with foil. Bake in preheated 350°F oven covered for 20 minutes. Remove cover. Spread remaining cheese on top of enchiladas. Bake uncovered 5 minutes or until cheese melts. Serve with chopped green onion sprinkled on top.

Serves 4 – 6

Chicken Fajitas

Terri Grimes, Indianapolis Indiana

If your prefer you can make these fajitas with beef instead of chicken. To really kick it up try a mixture of beef and chicken.

¼ cup fresh lime juice	1 green pepper, cut in strips
1 clove garlic, finely minced	1 medium onion, cut in wedges
1 teaspoon chili powder	12 flour tortillas
½ teaspoon cumin	½ cup salsa
2 boneless, skinless chicken breasts	1 ½ cups shredded cheddar cheese
2 tablespoons olive oil	½ cup sour cream
1 red pepper, cut in strips	

In medium glass bowl mix lime juice, garlic, chili powder and cumin. Cut chicken in thin strips and add to lime mixture. Marinade 15 to 30 minutes. Sauté, chicken in oil until no longer pink. Add peppers and onion. Sauté 3 to 5 minutes more. Divide chicken evenly among tortillas. Top with salsa, cheese and sour cream. Roll up and serve.

Serves 4

Chicken Piccata

Terri Grimes, Indianapolis Indiana

I told my husband that only I could make chicken piccata taste this good. He tried to do a good deed and cook dinner one night. He made my famous chicken piccata and it was just as good as mine. I was not happy. The moral that he learned? No good deed is left unpunished.

1 pound boneless skinless chicken breasts

2 tablespoons olive oil

¼ cup white wine

1 teaspoon minced garlic

½ cup chicken broth

2 tablespoons fresh lemon juice

2 tablespoons capers, drained

2 tablespoons butter

fresh lemon slices

¼ cup chopped parsley (optional)

Pound chicken breasts until they are thin cutlets. (I use a rolling pin) You may have to cut them in half prior to pounding if they are thick chicken breasts. Some grocery stores sell thin chicken cutlets. Season chicken with salt and pepper to taste. Sauté chicken in 2 tablespoons olive oil in large nonstick skillet. Remove chicken from pan. Deglaze pan with white wine and minced garlic for approximately 3 minutes or until wine is reduced. Add lemon juice and capers. Return cutlets to pan and cook 1 minute per side. Remove cutlets. Finish sauce by placing butter and lemon slices in pan. Cook over medium heat for 2 minutes. Pour sauce over chicken cutlets. Garnish with fresh parsley and serve.

Serves 4

Chicken Stirfry

Greg Grimes, Indianapolis Indiana

This is the first dish I cooked for Terri when we were dating. I think this meal is how I won her heart. Every couple of months I will make this Stirfry for her to remind her how much I love her. I make her chop the veggies though.

1 pound boneless, skinless chicken breast

1 tablespoons soy sauce

1 tablespoon sesame oil

2 tablespoons peanut oil (or olive oil)

2 large cloves garlic, minced

1 tablespoon minced ginger

1 red bell pepper, chopped

1 small yellow summer squash, sliced

1 small onion, chopped

1 cup sliced mushrooms

½ cup snow peas

2 medium carrots, peeled and sliced

One 8-ounce can sliced water chestnuts, drained

¼ cup Hoisin

2 tablespoons soy sauce

1 tablespoon rice wine vinegar

2 teaspoons Thai chili sauce

¼ cup white wine

1/ cup chicken broth

2 tablespoons cornstarch

3 tablespoons water

Dice chicken in bite size pieces. Place in bowl with 1 tablespoon soy sauce and sesame oil. Set aside to marinate at least 15 minutes while you prepare the vegetables. In a hot wok or large nonstick skillet sauté garlic and ginger in peanut oil for 1 minute. Add chicken and stir-fry 3 minutes or until chicken is browned on all sides. Add vegetables. Cover wok or skillet and cook 3 to 5 minutes or until veggies are tender crisp. In bowl combine hoisin, 2 tablespoons soy sauce, rice wine vinegar, chili sauce, wine, chicken broth, cornstarch and water. Pour over vegetables. Simmer uncovered 3 minutes or until sauce is hot, bubbly and thickened. Serve over rice.

Serves 4 to 6

Chicken with Lemon and Green Onion Sauce

Terri Grimes, Indianapolis Indiana

Chicken breasts are absolutely delicious broiled then served with this wonderful sauce. If you can find organic, free-range chicken, it's great with this sauce.

4 boneless chicken breast halves	*2 green onions, chopped*
Olive oil (to rub on chicken)	*1 clove garlic, minced*
4 tablespoons butter	*1 teaspoon chopped fresh parsley*
2 tablespoons lemon juice	*½ teaspoon salt*
½ teaspoon lemon zest	*¼ teaspoon black pepper*

Preheat broiler. Put chicken breast between two sheets of wax paper and pound to thin to an even thickness. Rub with olive oil and sprinkle with salt and pepper. Arrange on oiled broiler rack. In saucepan, combine remaining ingredients and bring to boil. Reduce heat and simmer 1 minute. Broil chicken till done, about 6 minutes per side. Drizzle each breast with lemon mixture 1 minute before chicken is done. Serve chicken with the remaining sauce.

Serves 4.

Crunchy Tenders

Terri Grimes, Indianapolis Indiana

1 ½ pound chicken breast tenders	*¼ cup flour*
Salt and pepper to taste	*1 cup Panko (Japanese Breadcrumbs)*
1 egg, beaten	*Peanut oil, for frying (or canola)*

Salt and pepper chicken tenders. Dust seasoned chicken with flour. Dip chicken in beaten egg. Coat chicken thoroughly with Panko. Either pan fry or deep fry in hot peanut oil until golden. Serve with a dipping sauce such as sweet and sour sauce, honey mustard or your favorite BBQ sauce.

Serves 4

Easy Chicken Marinade

Linda Ilsley, Topanga California

This marinade is also great on pork. I like to put the chicken in this marinade in the morning, and throw them on the grill at dinner time or an easy meal.

¼ cup soy sauce

¼ cup brown sugar

¼ cup dijon mustard

1 pound chicken breasts

Whisk together soy sauce, brown sugar and mustard. Pour over chicken. Allow to marinate at least a couple of hours before grilling or broiling.

Serves 4

Lemon Garlic Chicken

Terri Grimes, Indianapolis Indiana

I created this recipe years ago when my kids were little tots. This chicken is not only extremely flavorful, but it also makes the most tender chicken you have ever put in your mouth. I like to serve it with rice so we can spoon the flavorful juices over the rice. This dish is a family favorite.

1 whole frying chicken, cut in serving pieces

Juice of 4 fresh lemons

2 tablespoons olive oil

12 cloves garlic, minced

½ teaspoon kosher salt

½ teaspoon black pepper

¼ cup chopped fresh curly parsley

In 2 quart casserole dish combine all ingredients, tossing to combine. Cover and place in refrigerator at least 8 hours, or preferably overnight. Stir every couple of hours. Keeping dish covered, bake at 300°F for 1 hour. Remove cover and bake an additional 30 minutes.

Serves 4

Naked Chef Chicken

Greg Grimes, Indianapolis Indiana

My family dubbed this 'Naked Chef Chicken' because my recipe was inspired by a cooking method used by Jamie Oliver, the Naked Chef. Don't worry, there is no nudity involved in the making of this dish...most of the time.

1 whole chicken, cut in serving pieces	*1 tablespoon fresh rosemary, minced*
3 – 4 medium potatoes, cut in wedges	*1 tablespoon fresh thyme*
3 medium carrots, peeled and sliced	*1 tablespoon fresh sage, minced*
2 medium parsnips, peeled and sliced	*1 tablespoon dried basil*
1 large onion, cut in chunks	*1 teaspoon kosher salt*
12 cloves garlic, peeled	*1 teaspoon black pepper*
1 lemon	*¼ cup white wine*
2 tablespoons olive oil	

Preheat oven to 400°F. In roasting pan combine chicken, vegetables and garlic. Drizzle olive oil over mixture, tossing to coat. Squeeze lemon juice over chicken and veggie mixture, tossing to coat. Take lemon rind and cut in 1-inch pieces. Add to chicken/veggie mixture. In small bowl combine rosemary, thyme, sage, bail, salt and pepper. Sprinkle herbs over chicken/veggie mixture, tossing well to distribute herbs evenly throughout. Spread chicken and veggies evenly in roasting pan in one layer. Drizzle white wine over mixture. You do not need to toss. Bake 1 hour, stirring chicken/veggie mixture every 20 minutes for even browning.

Serves 4 to 6

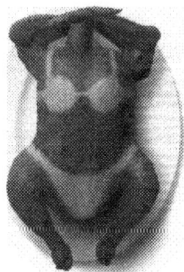

Sesame Sweet Chicken

Terri Grimes, Indianapolis Indiana

3 pounds boneless skinless chicken

½ cup hoisin

½ cup honey

3 tablespoons lime juice

2 tablespoons soy sauce

1 tablespoon minced ginger

1 tablespoon sesame seeds

½ teaspoon cumin

½ teaspoon paprika

Combine hoisin, honey, lime juice and soy sauce. Stir in ginger, sesame seeds, cumin and paprika. Reserve ¼ cup marinade. Marinade chicken in sauce for a minimum of 1 hour, preferably overnight. Turn chicken occasionally. Bake, broil or grill chicken until juices run clear, spreading with reserved sauce halfway through.

Serves 6 to 8

Steamed Cornish Hens

Cindy Newsom, Walker Louisiana

2 Cornish Hens

1 teaspoon garlic powder

1 teaspoon onion powder

1 teaspoon Season All

½ teaspoon ground sage

Preheat oven to 350°F. Mix seasonings together and set aside. Use heavy-duty aluminum foil sheets approximately 2 feet long. Put one hen on each sheet of foil. Season the hens liberally with the seasonings mixture. Wrap the seasoned hens loosely to form a 'tent' around the hens. Place them on a cookie sheet. Bake 50 to 55 minutes. Open the 'tents' carefully because of escaping steam and be careful not to spill the juices. Put back in the oven for approximately 10 minutes just to brown the tops of the hens. Serve and enjoy!

Serves 2

Szechwan Chicken

Terri Grimes, Indianapolis Indiana

Use this marinade for things other than chicken. I marinade vegetables in the spicy concoction before threading onto skewers to grill. Make sure you don't cross contaminate though, so reserve the portion of marinade for your vegetables before placing chicken in marinade. Another favorite is tuna steaks. Don't marinate the tuna any longer than 30 minutes, however, or it will become too tender and fall apart.

¼ cup soy sauce

2 tablespoons sesame oil

2 tablespoons vegetable oil

2 tablespoons tomato paste

1 tablespoon fresh lemon juice

¼ cup orange juice

2 tablespoons orange zest

1 tablespoon fresh grated ginger

2 large cloves garlic, finely minced

½ teaspoon pepper

1 pound boneless skinless chicken breasts

Using a glass or plastic bowl (not metal) mix all ingredients, except chicken. Marinate chicken one hour prior to cooking. You can use whole chicken breasts or cut boneless skinless chicken breasts into 1-inch pieces and thread on skewers. If making kabobs, be sure to marinate vegetables in a separate bowl of marinade to avoid cross contamination. Chicken soaked in this marinade is excellent cooked on the grill.

Serves 4

Baby Back Ribs

Greg Grimes, Indianapolis Indiana

Whether you use your oven, grill or smoker, the secret to a good rib is 'slow and low'. Follow that rule your ribs will turn out great every time.

2 racks of baby-back ribs

¼ cup of dry rub (found on the spice aisle)

8 ounces of your favorite barbecue sauce

1 teaspoon Worcestershire sauce

Salt and pepper, several dashes of each

Preheat oven to 275°F. Dust both sides of the ribs with rub, salt and pepper. Place in roasting pan, fat side up. Place in oven for 2 ½ hours. (or until tender). Remove from oven. In a bowl, add Worcestershire sauce to barbecue sauce and mix well. Preheat grill. Coat one side of ribs with sauce and lightly brown that side over moderate heat in covered grill (approximately 5 minutes). Coat the other side and turn, browning another 5 minutes. Remove from grill and serve.

Serves 4

Bowtie Pasta with Basil Cream Sauce

Terri Grimes, Indianapolis Indiana

6-ounces bowtie pasta

1 cup frozen peas, thawed

12-ounce can light evaporated milk

1 tablespoon cornstarch

1 clove garlic, finely minced

2 tablespoons fresh basil minced

2-ounces deli ham, chopped

¼ cup grated Parmesan

2 tablespoons grated Parmesan

1 tomato, seeded and chopped

Cook pasta according to package directions. Meanwhile combine milk and cornstarch in a medium saucepan. Mix in garlic and basil. Cook over medium heat until thickened and bubbly. Add thawed peas, cooking one minute more. Add ham and ¼ cup Parmesan. Stir over low heat until cheese is melted. Add tomatoes and pour over cooked pasta. Top with 2 tablespoons Parmesan.

Serves 2

Broccoli & Ham Quiche

Cindy Newsom, Walker Louisiana

Great for Leftover Ham!

1 pie crust

3 large eggs

½ cup instant mashed potato flakes, divided

One 9-ounce package frozen broccoli, thawed

¾ cup cooked ham, diced

One 10-ounce can cream of celery soup

1 tablespoon Dijon mustard

1 clove garlic, pressed

2 teaspoons Dill mix

¾ cup shredded Swiss or cheddar cheese, grated

8 cherry tomatoes (optional)

Additional dill (optional)

Preheat oven to 400°F. Let piecrust stand at room temperature 15 minutes. Unfold crust onto large cutting board; roll lightly to smooth seams and form an even circle. Place crust in deep baking dish, pressing dough into bottom and up sides. Beat eggs in small bowl. Brush pastry crust lightly with some of the egg mixture. Sprinkle half of the potato flakes evenly over bottom of crust. Coarsely chop broccoli. In medium bowl, combine broccoli, ham, soup, mustard, pressed garlic, remaining potato flakes and 2 Tablespoons dill; mix well. Microwave filling on High 4 minutes or until hot. Add egg mixture to broccoli mixture; stir well. Add cheese to broccoli mixture; mix well. Pour filling into baking dish over crust, spreading evenly. Decoratively flute edge of crust. If desired, cut cherry tomatoes in half; arrange, cut sides up, over filling in a circular pattern. Sprinkle tomato halves with additional dill, if desired. Bake 35-40 minutes or until light golden brown and set in center.

Serves 4 to 6

Easy BBQ Pork Sandwich

Terri Grimes, Indianapolis Indiana

Serve hot with plenty of napkins. Great with coleslaw on the side.

1 cup water

2 teaspoons cider vinegar

1 bay leaf

1 clove garlic, minced

2 teaspoons oil

4 boneless pork cutlets, 1/4-inch thick

4 Kaiser rolls

1 ½ cups barbeque sauce

Put water, vinegar, bay leaf, and garlic in large saucepan and heat but do not boil. In deep skillet heat oil. Sear cutlets on each side (about 1 minute per side). Pour hot water/vinegar mixture on top of cutlets. Simmer, covered, about 30 minutes or until pork is fork tender. Pour barbeque sauce into skillet and heat on medium-low. Split rolls, and lightly toast. Put one cutlet on each roll and spoon on as much warm sauce as you want.

Serves 4

Grilled Ham Steak

Terri Grimes, Indianapolis Indiana

¼ cup apricot preserves

1 tablespoon mustard

1 teaspoon lemon juice

1/8 teaspoon cinnamon

One 2-pound ham steak, 1-inch thick

Combine preserves, mustard, lemon juice and cinnamon in small saucepan. Simmer over low heat 5 minutes or until preserves are melted. Score the fat on the edges of the ham steak. Grill 8-10 minutes, turning half-way through cooking time. Brush with glaze during last few minutes of cooking. This can also be cooked on the broiler or oven.

Serves 2

Red Beans and Rice

Greg Grimes, Indianapolis Indiana

This is normally served on Mondays in New Orleans, as that was traditionally "Wash Day". When the laundry was done so were the beans. Others say that this dish was served on Mondays because it used Sunday's ham bone. Either way it is a delicious and easy dish. Enjoy!

1 pound dry red kidney beans	*1 smoked ham hock*
2 quarts water	*1 pound andouille sausage*
4 tablespoons olive oil	*2 bay leaves*
1 large onion, chopped	*1 teaspoon cayenne pepper*
1 large green pepper, chopped	*1 teaspoon kosher salt*
3 stalks celery, chopped	*1/8 teaspoon black pepper*
2 large cloves garlic, minced	*Steamed rice*

Soak beans overnight in enough water to cover at least 1-inch above beans. Drain beans. Place beans and 2 quarts water in a large pot. Bring just to a boil. Immediately turn down to a simmer. In the meantime sauté onion, green pepper, celery and garlic in olive oil 3 – 5 minutes. Slice sausage into ½-inch pieces. Add to vegetables and sauté an additional 3 minutes or until vegetables are soft. Add vegetable/sausage mixture and ham hock into beans that have just come to a boil. Add the bay leaves, cayenne pepper, salt and black pepper. Simmer 2 to 3 hours. Serve over rice.

Serves 6

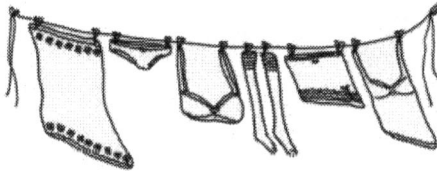

Crab Cakes

Terri Grimes, Indianapolis Indiana

If you like Maryland crab cakes, you will love this classic recipe featuring fresh lump crab meat that is sensationally seasoned with Old Bay Seasoning. This is a staple where I hail from.

2 slices white bread, crusts removed and crumbled

2 tablespoons mayonnaise

2 teaspoons Old Bay Seasoning

2 teaspoons chopped fresh parsley

1/2 teaspoon prepared yellow mustard

1 egg, beaten

1 pound fresh lump crabmeat

Mix bread, mayonnaise, Old Bay, parsley, mustard and egg in large bowl until well blended. Gently fold in crabmeat. Shape into 4 patties. Broil 10 minutes without turning or fry until golden brown on both sides. Dust with additional Old Bay, if desired.

Serves 4

Crawfish Etouffee'

Cindy Newsom, Walker Louisiana

1 pound crawfish tails (with fat on)

3-ounces tomato paste (optional)

One 10 ¾-ounce can Cream of Mushroom soup

One 10 ¾-ounce can Cream of Celery soup

½ package Chef's Seasoning ***

1 Stick Butter

1/8 teaspoon Cayenne pepper (optional)

In saucepan melt seasoning and butter. Add tomato paste, then add the crawfish. Let mixture simmer for a while. Add soups. Add a little cayenne pepper (also optional). Serve over rice. ***Chef's Seasoning (found in frozen foods section of your grocery).

Serves 4

Salmon Steaks

Jennifer Macaire, Montchauvet France

As a busy author writing books such as *Horse Passages, Virtual Murder*, and *Angels on Crusade*, just to name a few, I thrive on serving easy yet impressive dishes like this. An added bonus is while this recipe is a breeze to make; it's also a breeze to clean up. Just toss the foil in the garbage bin and cleanup is complete! I enjoy serving this Salmon with wild rice and a green salad. Reserve a small bowl of soy/maple syrup mixture to serve with the salmon.

Four 4-ounce Salmon steaks   *½ cup soy sauce*

½ cup maple syrup

Preheat oven to 400°F. Cut 4 pieces of foil. In center of each place 1 salmon steak. In bowl mix soy sauce and maple syrup. Mix well. Drizzle approximately 2 tablespoons of soy/syrup mixture over each salmon steak. Close foil to make individual packets. Bake 20 – 25 minutes.

Serves 4

Scalloped Oysters

Lottie Smith, Salisbury Maryland

Terri's Note: Grandmom would serve this dish at Christmas dinner along with about 50 other dishes on her huge buffet. She would only use freshly shucked oysters from Chincoteague Island.

1 quart shucked oysters in their liquor	*¾ cup melted butter*
2 cups coarsely-crushed saltine crackers	*1 cup cream*
1 cup dry bread crumbs	*Salt and pepper to taste*

Preheat oven to 350°F. Mix together crackers, bread crumbs and melted butter. Place a thin layer of crumb mixture in the bottom of buttered casserole dish. Cover with half of the oysters. Season cream with salt, and pepper. Pour half of this mixture over the oysters. On the next layer, use the oysters, 3/4 of the remaining crumb mixture and cover that with seasoned cream. Top with the remaining crumbs. Bake for 20 to 25 minutes, or until lightly browned.

Serves 6

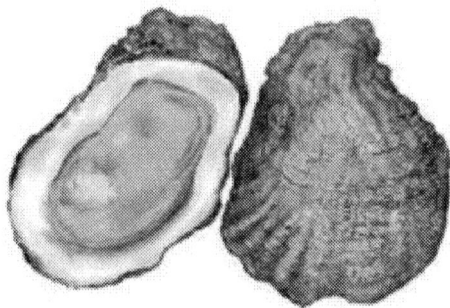

Shrimp Skewers with Fruit Salsa

Terri Grimes, Indianapolis Indiana

This makes for an impressive and easy dinner when company comes. This salsa is also excellent served over grilled swordfish or salmon.

Salsa:

1 ripe plum, chopped

2 apricots, diced

1 nectarine, diced

2 tablespoons thinly sliced fresh mint

2 tablespoons diced red onion

1 jalapeno, minced and seeded

1 teaspoon fresh lime zest

3 tablespoons fresh lime juice

1 tablespoon honey

1/4 teaspoon salt

1/8 teaspoon ground red pepper

12 sweet cherries, pitted and halved

1 green onion, finely chopped

Shrimp:

2 tablespoons butter, melted

2 teaspoons fresh lemon juice

1/4 teaspoon salt

1 garlic clove, minced

24 jumbo shrimp, peeled and deveined (about 2 pounds)

Cooking spray

6 lime wedges

To prepare salsa, combine all of the salsa ingredients in a medium bowl; stir well. Cover and chill 1 hour. To prepare shrimp, place butter, 2 teaspoons juice, 1/4 teaspoon salt, garlic, and shrimp in a large bowl; toss to coat. Thread 6 shrimp onto each of 4 (12-inch) skewers. Place kebabs on a grill rack coated with cooking spray; grill for 3 minutes on each side or until shrimp are done. Serve with salsa and lime wedges.

Serves 4.

Vegetable and Side Dishes

Baked Basil Fries

Baked Eggplant Mozzarella

Basil Cherry Tomatoes

Boston Baked Beans

Carrot Raisin Salad

Collard Greens

Corn Fritters

Corn Pudding

Cowboy Beans

Damned Good Stuffing

Decadent Mac and Cheese

Deviled Eggs

Easy Mac and Cheese

Fried Corn

Green Bean Casserole

Grilled Spicy Potatoes

Hash Brown Casserole

O'Brien Potatoes

Ol' No. 7 Sweet Potatoes

Orange Ginger Carrots

Orange Sweet Potatoes
Pineapple Casserole
Rice Pilaf
Scalloped Potatoes
Squash Fritters
Squash Pudding
Zucchini Medley

Baked Basil Fries

Kate Chaplin, Indianapolis Indiana

1/8 cup grated parmesan cheese

½ tablespoon olive or vegetable oil

½ tablespoon dried basil

1/8 teaspoon garlic powder

2 medium red potatoes

Preheat oven to 425°F. In a bowl, combine Parmesan, oil, basil and garlic powder. Cut potatoes into ¼ inch sticks. Add cheese mixture, toss and coat. Place in a 15x10 pan coated with non-stick spray. Bake 15 minutes; turn potatoes. Bake 15-20 minutes or until crisp and tender.

Serves 2

Baked Eggplant Mozzarella

Terri Grimes, Indianapolis Indiana

This recipe is from a magazine clipping dated 1942. Even people that don't like eggplant can't help but like this dish.

½ cup flour

1 egg

1/3 cup milk

¼ teaspoon pepper

1 large eggplant, cut into 1/3-inch slices

4 tablespoons olive oil

1 pound mozzarella, sliced thin

16-ounces spaghetti sauce

½ cup parmesan cheese

Preheat oven to 375°F. Put flour in a bag. In bowl beat egg, milk and pepper. Put 3 or 4 slices of eggplant in the bag of flour. Close bag and shake well. Heat 1 tablespoon oil in skillet. Dip floured eggplant in milk mixture. Fry till brown on both sides. Drain on paper towels. Repeat until of eggplant is fried. Arrange half of eggplant in an 11x7-inch baking dish. Top eggplant with ½ of mozzarella. Top with ½ of spaghetti sauce. Top with ½ of parmesan cheese. Repeat. Bake uncovered 40 minutes.

Serves 4

Basil Cherry Tomatoes

Kate Chaplin, Indianapolis Indiana

2 pints cherry tomatoes, halved

½ cup chopped fresh basil

1 ½ teaspoons olive or vegetable oil

Onion powder to taste

Garlic salt to taste

Salt and pepper to taste

Place cherry tomato halves in a salad bowl. Combine basil, oil and seasonings. Toss and serve.

Serves 4 to 6

Boston Bakes Beans

United States Navy, USA

This is from a regulation cookbook given to United States Navy messmen in 1944. What would the Navy be without its beans?

12 pounds dried navy beans

Cold water, to cover

3 to 4 Gallons Water, boiling

5-ounces Salt

1-ounce dry mustard

4 pounds salt pork, bacon, or ham fat, cubed

1-quart molasses

Pick over and wash beans thoroughly. Soak in cold water about 6 hours. Do not drain. Add boiling water to cover. Simmer about 1 hour until beans are tender, but not mushy. Drain off excess liquid. Reserve. Add salt, mustard, salt pork and molasses. Place in baking pans. Bake in slow oven (300° F) 3 to 4 hours, adding liquid from the boiled beans as needed.

Serves 100

Carrot Raisin Salad

Terri Grimes, Indianapolis Indiana

This is a yummy old fashioned salad that packs great flavor any time of the year. Lots of crunch with a pleasing sweetness.

4 cups peeled, grated carrots (4 to 5 large carrots)

¾ cup raisins

¼ cup mayonnaise

2 tablespoons sugar

2 to 3 tablespoons milk

Place carrots and raisins in a large bowl. In a small bowl whisk together salad dressing, sugar and enough milk to achieve the consistency of a creamy salad dressing. Pour over carrot mixture and toss to coat well.

Serves 8

Collard Greens

Greg Grimes, Indianapolis Indiana

2 quarts water

1 smoked ham hock

½ teaspoon garlic salt

¼ teaspoon red pepper flakes

2 tablespoons apple cider vinegar

2 pounds fresh collard greens, stems picked and removed

1 small onion, chopped

2 cloves garlic, minced

1 tablespoon butter

In a large pot, bring 2 quarts of water to a boil. Add ham hock, garlic salt, red pepper flakes and vinegar. Reduce heat to medium; simmer 30 minutes. Meanwhile, wash collard greens. Remove the stems that run down the center of each leaf. Stack 6 to 8 leaves on top of one another, roll up, and slice into 1/2- to 1-inch thick slices. Place greens in pot with meat. Sauté onion and garlic in butter 3 to 5 minutes or until onions are soft. Add onions and garlic to greens. Simmer 2 hours or longer, stirring occasionally. When done taste and adjust seasoning with salt and pepper to taste.

Serves 4 to 6

Corn Fritters

Terri Grimes, Indianapolis Indiana

2 cups flour	*1/8 teaspoon pepper*
One 15-ounce can whole kernel corn	*1 large egg*
2 teaspoons baking powder	*¾ cup milk*
1 teaspoon Salt	*1 tablespoon butter*

In a mixing bowl, sift together the flour, baking powder, pepper and salt. In a separate small mixing bowl beat the egg. Drain the corn saving ¼ cup of the liquid. Add the corn, milk, softened butter and the ¼ cup liquid drained from the corn. Mix thoroughly then add this to the flour mixture and continue mixing. Heat about 1-½ inches of vegetable oil in a deep pan or wok. Drop the fritter dough by spoonfuls into the hot oil and cook until golden brown, turning them while they are cooking to get browned on all sides.

Serves 6

Corn Pudding

Terri Grimes, Indianapolis Indiana

½ cup sugar	*2 large eggs*
3 tablespoons cornstarch	*One 12-ounce can evaporated milk*
One 15-ounce can cream style corn	*¼ teaspoon vanilla*

Preheat oven to 350°F. Grease a 1-1/2 quart baking dish. Combine all of the above and mix well. Turn into baking dish and dot with butter. Bake about one hour or until center is almost firm. Let stand ten minutes prior to serving. Delicious!

Serves 6

Cowboy Beans

Terri Grimes, Indianapolis Indiana

Greg and I followed the competition BBQ circuit for several years and even bottled our own rubs and BBQ sauces for resale. Every team in the circuit has their own signature recipes for side dishes and often fights for bragging rights over those side dishes. Every BBQ team swears their bean dish is the best. Actually ours is the best bean recipe you'll find!

1 pound dried pinto beans*	*1/2 teaspoon chili powder*
5 cups Water	*1/2 teaspoon paprika*
1 cup apple juice	*1/2 teaspoon cumin*
1 cup beer (we like to use a dark beer)	*1/2 teaspoon ground ginger*
	1/4 teaspoon celery salt

Bring beans just to a boil. Remove from heat and allow to soak overnight or at least 6 hours. Cook bacon in skillet and place on paper towels to drain. After bacon cools, crumble. Add green pepper, onions, jalapeno and garlic to bacon drippings and sauté. Drain beans and add all ingredients. Cook till almost tender, pour into a disposable aluminum shallow pan and place in smoker or in oven. The skin that forms will need to be stirred in every 30 minutes until beans are tender. This is particularly important if you are smoking the beans on your smoker or grill. If cooking in oven bake at 350°F. If cooking on the smoker or grill 250°F to 300°F is desirable.

Serves 8

NOTE – Sometimes I use a large jar of the mixed beans that are already cooked, in place of the dried beans. (I think it's a quart sized jar)Just skip the soaking part if you use the jar or can of beans. Or you could mix several cans of beans. Mix different varieties like northern beans, pinto beans or just use 3 cans of pinto beans.

Damned Good Stuffing

Terri Grimes, Indianapolis Indiana

The first Thanksgiving I made this stuffing everyone kept raving "That is good stuffing, damned good stuffing!" They talked about it all afternoon and evening. When I walked into the kitchen the next morning I overheard my brother in law telling my husband "that was damned good stuffing". Now everyone reminds me at Thanksgiving to be sure to make that "Damned Good Stuffing".

9 cups bread crumbs, I prefer seasoned

1 pound mild sausage

2 cups chopped onions

¼ cup butter

2 tart apples, unpeeled, cored and chopped

1 cup pecans, chopped

1 teaspoon dried thyme

1 teaspoon rubbed sage

1 teaspoon poultry seasoning

½ teaspoon salt

¼ teaspoon pepper

½ cup apple juice

2 – 4 cups Chicken broth

Preheat oven to 325°F. Place bread crumbs in large bowl. In skillet sauté sausage, onion and butter until sausage is cooked. Do not drain. Add sausage mixture to bread crumbs and toss. Add apples, pecans and seasonings. Toss well. Stir in apple juice and enough chicken broth to moisten. Place in a greased 3 quart baking dish. Cover and bake 50 minutes. Remove cover and bake an additional 20 minutes to brown.

Serves 10

Decadent Mac and Cheese

Terri Grimes, Indianapolis Indiana

What better side dish than good old-fashioned macaroni and cheese! So versatile, it goes with everything. This recipe isn't as easy as opening a box of that crafty stuff, but I guarantee it tastes bunches better. Enjoy!

Vegetable oil

½ pound cavatappi

½ quart milk

5 tablespoons butter, divided

¼ cup all-purpose flour

6-ounces Gruyere, grated

4-ounces sharp white cheddar, grated

½ teaspoon black pepper

1 teaspoon Kosher salt

¼ teaspoon ground nutmeg

3 small fresh tomatoes

1 cup Panko (Japanese bread crumbs) or fresh white bread crumbs

Preheat the oven to 375°F. Drizzle oil into a large pot of boiling salted water. Add the macaroni and cook according to the directions on the package, 6 to 8 minutes. Drain well. Meanwhile, melt 3 tablespoons of butter in a large (4-quart) pot and add the flour. Cook, stirring constantly with whisk, over low heat for 2 minutes. While whisking, add the milk and cook for a minute or two more, until thickened and smooth. Once off the heat, add the Gruyere, Cheddar, salt, pepper, and nutmeg. Add the cooked macaroni and stir well. Pour into a greased 3-quart baking dish. Slice the tomatoes and arrange on top. Melt the remaining 2 tablespoons of butter, combine them with the fresh bread crumbs, and sprinkle on the top. Bake for 30 to 35 minutes, or until the sauce is bubbly and the macaroni is browned on the top.

Serves 6

Deviled Eggs

Cindy Newsom, Walker Louisiana

This is one of those items that I am always asked to bring to each and every gathering, from Thanksgiving Easter to July 4th.

1 ½ Dozen Eggs	*Pepper*
Items below are `to taste':	*Garlic powder*
Mayonnaise (NOT Miracle Whip)	*Onion powder*
Mustard	*Pickle relish (optional)*
Salt	*Paprika*

Place eggs in large pot and cover with cold water. Heat on highest setting till water comes to a boil. Boil eggs 15 minutes. Drain and cover with cold water to cool. Once cooled, peel eggs. Cut each egg in half the long way. Drop the yolk into a bowl and put the white half on an egg dish or platter. If the white is messed up, drop it in the bowl too. Mash the parts in the bowl (or use a food processor) and add all above ingredients (except the paprika). Fill each egg white half, with a spoon full of your egg mixture and top with paprika. Place a toothpick in each egg and cover with Saran Wrap until serving time. The toothpicks keep the wrap from mashing the eggs.

Serves 6 to 8

Easy Mac and Cheese

Terri Grimes, Indianapolis Indiana

We had a houseguest that stayed for six long weeks back in the late 90's. His only redeeming quality was this recipe. Our dog enjoyed his visit though, or maybe it was chewing on our houseguest's denture that our dog enjoyed.

8-ounces macaroni	*1 egg, beaten*
4-ounces sharp cheddar cheese, grated	*1 cup milk*
4-ounces Monterey Jack cheese, grated	*4 tablespoons butter*

Preheat oven to 350°F. Cook macaroni according to package directions. Drain well. Mix all ingredients, reserving a small amount of cheddar and Monterey cheese. Put mixture in a buttered 2 quart casserole dish. Sprinkle reserved cheese on top of dish. Bake 30 – 45 minutes or until top is golden.

Serves 4 to 6

Fried Corn

Terri Grimes, Indianapolis Indiana

This is about as Southern as it gets. If you hail from South of the Mason Dixon line you know what a treat this dish can be.

2 tablespoons butter	*1 tablespoon sugar*
½ cup finely chopped onion	*1 teaspoon salt*
½ cup finely chopped red bell pepper	*1 teaspoon black pepper*
One 16-ounce bag frozen white corn	

In a large skillet sauté onion and red pepper until slightly softened (about 4 minutes). Add the corn, sugar, salt and pepper. Sauté, stirring often, for approximately 10 minutes. Enjoy!

Serves 4 to 6

Green Bean Casserole

Brooke Houk, Schweinfurt Germany

Everyone has his or her own favorite comfort food dish at the holidays. This dish is my favorite.

¾ cup milk

½ teaspoon black pepper

One 10-ounce can cream of mushroom soup

Two 14-ounce cans cut green beans, drained

1 1/3 cup Durkee French fried onions

Preheat oven to 350°F. In 2 quart casserole dish combine all ingredients except 2/3 cup of the fried onions. Bake uncovered 30 minutes or until hot and bubbly. Top casserole with remaining fried onions. Bake 5 minutes more or until onions are golden.

Serves 6

Grilled Spicy Potatoes

Andrew Timmons, Indianapolis Indiana

My daughter, Jasmine, loves these potatoes and has been eating them since she was 3 years old. Everyone who tries them loves them.

4 medium potatoes, peeled and cut in 1-inch chunks

¼ cup hot sauce (I prefer Franks)

¼ cup (1/2 stick) butter, melted

1 teaspoon garlic salt

1 teaspoon lemon pepper

Salt and pepper to taste

Combine all ingredients, tossing well to coat potatoes. Place potato mixture on large square of heavy duty foil. Place another square of foil on top and seal edges to form a pouch. Place pouch on grill. Cook over indirect heat 30 to 40 minutes or until potatoes are tender.

Serves 4

Hash Brown Casserole

Terri Grimes, Indianapolis Indiana

I think my version of this classic tastes exactly like Cracker Barrel's rich, cheesy baked potato casserole. This is one of those perfect comfort foods.

One 10-ounce can cream of chicken soup

8-ounces Colby cheese, grated

½ cup melted butter

1 small onion, minced

1 teaspoon salt

½ teaspoon black pepper

2-pound bag frozen shredded hash browns

Preheat oven to 350°F. Grease a 13" X 9" baking pan. In bowl, combine soup, cheese, butter, onion, salt, and pepper. Gently fold potatoes into mixture and pour into prepared pan. Bake 40 minutes or until top is golden.

Yield 8 servings.

O'Brien Potatoes

Greg Grimes, Indianapolis Indiana

This is from a regulation cookbook given to United States Navy messmen in 1944. The Destroyer my father was on had 250 crewmen, so they needed 102 pounds of potatoes just for one meal with this recipe. Imagine peeling those!

44 pounds Potatoes

6 tablespoons salt

1 pound green peppers, chopped fine

1 pound, 6-ounces Pimentos, chopped

8-ounces butter or bacon fat

Wash, peel and cut potatoes into ¾ inch cubes. Cover with cold water. Let stand 1 hour. Drain. Dry in a cloth. Fry in hot fat at 350 degrees 4 minutes, or until evenly browned. Drain and sprinkle with salt. Fry pimentos and green peppers in fat 3 minutes. Combine potatoes, pimentos and green peppers.

Serves 100

Ol' No. 7 Sweet Potatoes

Terri Grimes, Indianapolis Indiana

These yams are a staple on our Thanksgiving table. We have tried many sweet potato recipes but this is our favorite. And the left over Jack Daniels is always a treat too. ☺

One 40-ounce can sweet potatoes

1 ½ cups juice from sweet potatoes (add water to make 1 ½ cups if needed)

1 cup apple juice or apple cider

3 tablespoons butter

Orange peel from 1 orange

1/3 cup brown sugar, packed

1/3 cup bourbon (No. 7 Jack Daniels recommended)

½ teaspoon nutmeg

1 teaspoon cinnamon

Drain juice from canned sweet potatoes. In measuring cup measure 1 ½ cups reserved juice from sweet potatoes. If needed add water to make 1 ½ cups. In 2-quart saucepan combine sweet potato juice, apple juice, butter, orange peel, brown sugar, bourbon, nutmeg and cinnamon. Bring to a boil, then reduce heat and simmer 30 - 45 minutes. Sauce should be slightly thickened. Preheat oven to 350°F. Place drained sweet potatoes in a 2 quart baking dish. Pour syrup over sweet potatoes. Bake uncovered 30 minutes. Enjoy!

Serves 6

Orange Ginger Carrots

Terri Grimes, Indianapolis Indiana

This dish turns carrot haters into carrot lovers. Greg didn't eat veggies before I came along. Now he loves most veggies, including carrots and zucchini.

1 pound carrots	*1 tablespoon sugar*
Zest of 1 orange	*½ teaspoon ginger*
1 tablespoon butter	

Peel carrots. Slice into thin rounds using a diagonal cut, or whatever shape you prefer. Place carrots in medium saucepan with orange zest, butter, sugar and ginger. Cover with water. Simmer for 20 minutes or until carrots are tender. Be sure to check water level often to make sure you don't burn carrots. You want most of the water to cook away. These carrots have such a nice sweet citrus flavor; kids won't realize it's good for them.

Serves 4

Orange Sweet Potatoes

Terri Grimes, Indianapolis Indiana

This was a Thanksgiving staple until a couple of years ago when I started making the Ol' No. 7 Sweet Potatoes. Now I have to alternate so everyone in the family can get their favorite sweet potato fix at the Holidays.

Two 17-ounce cans sweet potatoes, drained	*¼ cup orange juice*
	½ teaspoon cinnamon
¼ cup butter, melted	*1 ½ cup mini marshmallows*

Preheat oven to 350°F. Mix all ingredients, except marshmallows. Beat with an electric mixer until smooth. Place in buttered 2 quart casserole dish. Bake 20 minutes. Top with marshmallows. Bake an additional 5 to 10 minutes or until marshmallows are browned.

Serves 4 to 6

Pineapple Casserole

Terri Grimes, Indianapolis Indiana

This is wonderful paired with a holiday ham. I've even cut the amounts by half and made it on a weeknight with pork chops or ham steaks.

1 cup sugar

¼-pound (1 stick) butter

4 eggs

One 14-ounce can crushed pineapple

7 slices white bread, cubed

Preheat oven to 350°F. With electric mixer cream sugar and butter. Add eggs one at a time, beating well after each addition. Fold in crushed pineapple and bread cubes. Bake uncovered 1 hour.

Serves 4 to 6

Rice Pilaf

Terri Grimes, Indianapolis Indiana

1/3 cup minced onion

1 ½ cups raw rice

1/3 cup olive oil

4 cups water

2 chicken bouillon cubes

1 cup broccoli florets

1 cup cherry tomatoes

½ cup shredded mozzarella

Place bouillon and water in saucepan. Bring to a boil. Add broccoli and simmer 5 minutes. Remove broccoli. Reserve water. Meanwhile sauté rice and onion in oil till light golden. Add 3 cups of the broccoli water to the rice mixture. Simmer covered until the liquid is absorbed and rice is tender. Add broccoli and tomatoes. Simmer 3 more minutes. Add mozzarella and serve.

Serves 4

Scalloped Potatoes

Terri Grimes, Indianapolis Indiana

This is such an easy side dish and makes the tastiest scalloped potatoes ever. You will never go back to the boxed kind after tasting these. For a different taste I will use a different cheese occasionally.

2 pounds potatoes, sliced thinly

½ cup melted butter

6-ounces Gruyere *cheese, grated*

Salt and pepper to taste

Preheat oven to 375°F. In greased 2-quart casserole dish place a layer of potatoes. Drizzle small amount of melted butter over top. Sprinkle salt and pepper over layer. Sprinkle small amount of cheese over that layer of potatoes. Repeat until all potatoes are used. Cover with foil. Bake 45 minutes. Remove foil cover. Bake an additional 20 minutes or until top is golden brown.

Serves 4 to 6

Squash Fritters

Terri Grimes, Indianapolis Indiana

You can make this with only zucchini or only squash. We prefer having a mixture of the two types. Whole kernel corn can be substituted for the squash.

2 medium zucchini or squash

½ cup flour

¼ cup milk

1 tablespoon sugar

2 eggs

1 teaspoon baking powder

Salt and pepper to taste

Oil for frying

Grate and drain squash and zucchini. Beat eggs then add to squash. Mix in all ingredients except cooking oil. Put 2 or 3 tablespoons cooking oil in hot skillet. Spoon onto hot skillet. Fry on both sides until golden brown.

Serves 4

Squash Pudding

Cindy Newsom, Walker Louisiana

6 medium squash (any kind) peeled and sliced

5-6 slices white Bread

1 cup milk

2 eggs, beaten

5 tablespoons Sugar

3 tablespoons butter, melted

Boil squash in saucepan 15 to 20 minutes until soft. Drain and let cool. Soak 3 slices of bread in the milk. Mix everything together adding the rest of the bread slices torn into pieces. Spread in baking dish (15 x 9 x 2). Bake at 400°F, until golden brown, approximately 45 minutes. This can be used as a desert (because of its sweetness) or as a side vegetable dish.

Serves 6 to 8

Zucchini Medley

Terri Grimes, Indianapolis Indiana

This dish turned my veggie-hating husband into a zucchini lover. It is one of his favorite veggie dishes in the summer when fresh zucchini is abundant.

1 medium green zucchini

1 medium yellow summer squash

½ cup onion, sliced

1 tablespoon olive oil

1 medium tomato, cut into 8 wedges

2 cloves garlic, minced

1 teaspoon basil

1 teaspoon oregano

½ teaspoon pepper

1 teaspoon kosher salt

Cut zucchini and squash into thin round slices. In nonstick skillet sauté zucchini, squash and onion in olive oil over medium heat for 2 minutes. Add in garlic and seasonings. Sauté 5 minutes until zucchini and squash are tender. Add tomato wedges and sauté 1-2 minutes or until tomatoes are heated through. Serve immediately.

Serves 4

Breads

Buddy's Cornbread

Buttermilk Biscuits

Cheese Biscuits

Cherry Applesauce Bread

Cinnabon Buns

Cloverleaf Potato Rolls

Cranberry Nut bread

Crawfish Cornbread

Focaccia

Fried Biscuits

Hushpuppies

Lottie's Cornbread

Morning Muffins

Soft Pretzels

Sweet Potato Biscuits

Zucchini Bread

Buddy's Cornbread

Terri Grimes, Indianapolis Indiana

This corn bread melts in your mouth, it is so good! I adapted it from a recipe similar to Buddy Guy's recipe (a Chicago Blues legend).

1 cup cornmeal* (make sure it is NOT cornmeal mix)

1 cup all-purpose flour

1/2 cup granulated sugar

1 tablespoon baking powder

1 teaspoon baking soda

1/4 teaspoon salt

1 large egg

4 tablespoons butter, melted

1 tablespoon shortening

1/2 cup buttermilk

1 cup 7-Up (you could use Sprite also)

Preheat oven to 350°F. Place a tablespoon of shortening in an iron skillet (about 10"-12" or 10" round cake pan) and place it in the preheated oven until the shortening is melted. By adding the cornbread batter to the hot shortening in the skillet, it gives it an excellent crust. Combine dry ingredients in a mixing bowl. Add liquid ingredients one at a time making sure 7-up is the last liquid ingredient you add. Mix with wire whisk until thoroughly combined. Fill hot skillet with cornbread batter. Bake 25 minutes or until top is golden brown. Brush top of cornbread generously with butter as soon as it comes out of the oven. Allow to cool approximately 10 minutes before cutting. ENJOY!

Serves 6 to 8

NOTE: Make sure you get plain cornmeal and not the cornmeal mix. If you do get the cornmeal mix just use 2 cups of it and omit the flour.

Buttermilk Biscuits

Greg Grimes, Indianapolis Indiana

I enjoy making these for our Sunday family dinners. They are light, fluffy and so good with a glob of butter and slathered with honey. One favorite menu to serve these with is Terri's fabulous fried chicken (made in an iron skillet) a fresh tossed green salad and hot fudge cake for dessert. Another reason to look forward to Sunday dinners!

2 cups all purpose flour (I like White Lilly)

2 teaspoons baking powder

½ teaspoon baking soda

½ teaspoon salt

¼ cup shortening

¾ cup buttermilk

1 egg

2 tablespoons water

Preheat oven to 425°F. Beat egg and water and set aside. This is called an "egg wash" and is used to give baked goods a golden sheen. Combine flour, baking powder, baking soda and salt. Cut in shortening using a pastry cutter or a fork. Stir in buttermilk to form a soft dough. Pat dough on a lightly floured board to a ½ inch thickness. Cut with a biscuit cutter. Place biscuits on ungreased baking sheet an inch apart. Lightly brush with egg wash. Bake 10-15 minutes or until golden.

Yield 10 to 12 biscuits

Cheese Biscuits

Terri Grimes, Indianapolis Indiana

2 cups self-rising flour

1 teaspoon baking powder

1 teaspoon sugar

1/3 cup shortening

3/4 cup grated sharp Cheddar

1 cup buttermilk

Dash salt

2 tablespoons butter, melted

Preheat oven to 350°F. In medium bowl, mix flour, baking powder, salt and sugar. Cut in shortening until it resembles cornmeal. Add cheese. Sir in buttermilk and mix until just blended. Do not over mix. Drop by generous spoonfuls on a greased baking sheet. Brush dough with melted butter. Bake 12 to 15 minutes. Brush with melted butter when done.

Yield 10 biscuits

Cherry Applesauce Bread

Terri Grimes, Indianapolis Indiana

1 cup dried cherries

1 cup applesauce

2 cups all purpose flour

1 teaspoon baking soda

¼ teaspoon salt

1 teaspoon cinnamon

1 teaspoon nutmeg

½ cup butter, softened to room temperature

½ cup sugar

½ cup brown sugar

1 egg

1 tablespoon orange zest

½ cup chopped pecans (optional)

Preheat oven to 325°F. Grease and flour a 9-inch loaf pan. Combine flour, baking soda, salt, cinnamon and nutmeg. In separate bowl cream butter with sugars until light and fluffy. Add egg and applesauce, mixing well. Mix flour mixture into butter mixture. Fold in cherries, orange zest and nuts. Place batter in loaf pan. Bake 50 minutes or until golden.

Yield 1 loaf

Cinnabon Buns

Greg Grimes, Indianapolis Indiana

Just like Cinnabon's cinnamon buns, only better! I make these yummy buns every Christmas morning for my family.

Rolls:

1 ¼-ounce packet active dry yeast

1 cup warm milk

½ cup granulated sugar

1/3 cup butter, melted

1 teaspoon salt

2 eggs

4 cups all-purpose flour

Filling:

1 cup packed brown sugar

2 ½ tablespoons cinnamon

1/3 cup butter, softened

Icing:

8 tablespoons (1 stick) butter, softened

1 ½ cups powdered sugar

¼ cup (2-ounces) cream cheese, softened

1 teaspoon vanilla extract

1/8 teaspoon salt

To make rolls, dissolve yeast in warm water in a large bowl. Add sugar, butter, salt, eggs and flour. Mix well. Knead dough into a large ball. Put in a bowl; cover and let rise in a warm place about an hour, or until dough has doubled in size. Roll dough out on lightly floured surface. Roll dough into a rectangle approximately 21-inches long by 16-inches wide. Dough should be about ¼-inch thick. Preheat oven to 400°F. Meanwhile prepare filling by combining brown sugar and cinnamon in a bowl. Spread softened butter evenly over surface of dough then sprinkle cinnamon sugar mixture evenly over top. Working from the top, (21-inch side) roll the dough in jellyroll fashion to the bottom edge. Cut rolled dough into 1 ¾-inch slices and place in a lightly greased baking sheet close together. Bake 10-15 minutes or until light brown on top. While rolls bake, make icing by combining all icing ingredients and beating on medium speed until light and fluffy. When rolls come out of oven coat each roll generously with icing. Enjoy!

Yield 12 large rolls

Cloverleaf Potato Rolls

Terri Grimes, Indianapolis Indiana

These are great for holiday meals and even regular family meals. The dough can be refrigerated for up to one week so you can take out as much as you need.

2 packages active dry yeast	*1 tablespoon salt*
½ cup warm water	*1 ½ cups scalded milk*
2 cups warm mashed potatoes	*2 eggs*
¾ cup butter, room temperature	*7 – 8 cups all-purpose flour*
½ cup sugar	

Soften yeast in warm water (110 degrees). Combine potatoes, butter, sugar, salt and hot milk. Cool to lukewarm. Add softened yeast and eggs. Stir in 4 cups flour and combine well. Stir in remaining flour, or enough to form a soft dough. Knead on lightly floured board till smooth and elastic. Place dough in greased bowl, turning to grease entire surface of dough. Cover with kitchen towel and let dough rise until double (about 1 hour). Punch down dough, shape into a ball and let rest for 10 minutes. At this point dough may be refrigerated for up to one week. Shape dough into cloverleaf rolls*, or shape desired. Let rise until double (about 1 hour). Bake in 400°F. As soon as you remove rolls from oven brush with melted butter to give rolls a nice sheen.

*To form cloverleaf rolls, grease a muffin pan. Roll 3 walnut sized balls of dough and place all three balls of dough into one muffin cup. Repeat until all muffin cups are filled with 3 balls of dough. Let rise until double and bake as directed.

Yield 4 dozen of the yummiest rolls you've ever eaten.

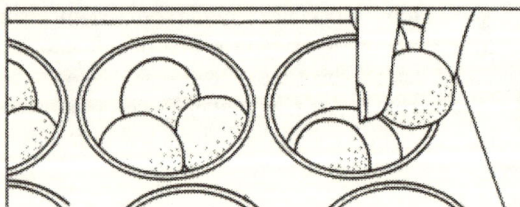

Cranberry Nut Bread

Terri Grimes, Indianapolis Indiana

This recipe makes great muffins. Just put batter into muffin tins instead of a loaf pan and reduce cooking time to 15 – 20 minutes. I buy extra bags of cranberries to freeze in the winter months when fresh cranberries are plentiful.

2 cups all-purpose flour

1 ½ teaspoons baking powder

½ teaspoon baking soda

1 teaspoon salt

1 cup sugar

¾ cup orange juice

1 tablespoon orange zest

1 teaspoon lemon zest

2 tablespoons butter, melted

1 large egg, beaten

1 teaspoon almond extract

2 tablespoons sugar (optional)

1 ½ cups fresh cranberries

½ cup chopped nuts (I use pecans)

Preheat oven to 350°F. Grease and flour a 9-inch loaf pan. Combine flour, baking powder, baking soda, salt and sugar. Stir in juice, zests, butter, egg and almond extract. Mix well. Chop cranberries coarsely. Fold cranberries and nuts into batter. I sprinkle batter with sugar for a wonderful finish. Bake 55 minutes.

Yield 1 loaf

Crawfish Cornbread

Cindy Newsom, Walker Louisiana

1 medium onion, chopped

½ cup oil

2 eggs

1 cup cornmeal

1 cup cheddar cheese, grated

1 teaspoon salt

1 teaspoon baking soda

¼ cup jalapeno peppers, chopped

One 15-ounce can creamed corn

1 pound crawfish tails, cooked and peeled

Preheat oven to 375°F. Mix all ingredients together. Pour into a greased 9 x 13 x 2" pan and bake 30 minutes.

Serves 4 to 6

Focaccia

Terri Grimes, Indianapolis Indiana

2 packets fast-rising dry yeast

2 cups water, at room temperature

2 tablespoons sugar

4 tablespoons olive oil

1/2 cup salad oil

1 teaspoons salt

5 1/2 cups bread flour

3 cloves garlic, crushed

1/4 cup olive oil, for topping

1 tablespoon rosemary, for topping

1 tablespoon kosher salt

Dissolve the yeast in water. Add sugar, olive oil, salad oil, and salt. Mix in 3 cups of flour and whip until dough begins to leave sides of the bowl, about 10 minutes. Mix in remaining flour by hand and knead dough until smooth. Allow dough to rise twice in the bowl and punch down after each rising. Oil two baking sheets, and divide the dough between the two pans. Using your fingers, press dough out to edge of each pan. Cover and let rise 30 minutes. Brush with a mixture of the crushed garlic and oil reserved for topping. Sprinkle with rosemary and salt. Bake in preheated 375°F oven 30 minutes.

Yield 2 Focaccia

Fried Biscuits

Terri Grimes, Indianapolis Indiana

When we moved to the Midwest we found that these are a Hoosier staple. After trying them we can definitely understand why.

One 10-ounce can refrigerated biscuits   *Vegetable oil for frying*

½ cup apple butter

Pour oil into deep fryer and heat to 350°F. Separate biscuits and fry 3 or 4 at a time in the hot oil. Cook 2 minutes (or until golden), turn over and cook the other side for 2 minutes (or until golden). Drain on paper towels. Serve warm with butter.

Yield 10 biscuits

Hushpuppies

Cindy Newsom, Walker Louisiana

3 cups cornmeal   *One 12-ounce can evaporated milk*

2 cups all-purpose flour   *½ cup water (approximate)*

1 tablespoon sugar   *3 eggs*

2 tablespoons baking powder   *Garlic powder to taste*

1 teaspoon salt   *Onion powder to taste*

Combine all dry ingredients. Stir in evaporated milk. Add only enough water to make batter a little thin. Stir until mixed well. Drop by spoonfuls into hot grease. Remove when golden brown. Put in brown bag. Hush puppies will remain crisp in brown bag if left open.

Yield 2 dozen

Lottie's Cornbread

Lottie Smith, Salisbury Maryland

Note from Terri: This recipe was my Grandmother's, Lottie Smith. She used to make this cornbread at least 3 times a week. She served homemade breads at every meal. This cornbread is almost pudding like. Cool before cutting.

2 cups yellow cornmeal	*½ cup sugar*
3 cups boiling water	*3 eggs, beaten*
3 tablespoons vegetable oil	*2 cups milk*
2 teaspoons salt	*1 tablespoon butter*

Preheat oven to 425°F. Pour cornmeal, oil, salt and sugar into a large mixing bowl. Pour boiling water over cornmeal mixture and beat with wooden spoon. Add milk and continue to beat. Add eggs and continue to beat until well combined. Put butter in iron skillet and place in preheated oven until skillet is hot and butter is melted. Immediately pour cornbread mixture into hot iron skillet. Bake 40 minutes. Cornbread will firm up as it cools.

Serves 6 to 8

Morning Muffins

Terri Grimes, Indianapolis Indiana

Homemade carrot cake inspired these moist and tender muffins. Made the night before, they are great for breakfast on the run.

1-1/2 cups all-purpose flour

1 cup quick Oats, uncooked

1/2 cup brown sugar, packed

1 tablespoon baking powder

1/2 teaspoon baking soda

1/2 teaspoon salt

1 tsp ground cinnamon

1/3 cup raisins

One 8-ounce can crushed pineapple, un-drained

1/2 cup carrots, shredded

1/2 cup skim milk

1/3 cup vegetable oil

2 egg whites, lightly beaten

1/3 cup powdered sugar (for glaze)

3 to 4 teaspoons skim milk (for glaze)

Heat oven to 400°F. Line 12 medium muffin cups with paper baking cups or lightly coat bottoms only with vegetable spray. Combine dry ingredients and raisins; mix well. Add combined pineapple, including juice, carrots, milk, oil and egg whites. Add to dry ingredients and mix just until dry ingredients are moistened. Fill muffin cups almost full. Bake 20 to 22 minutes or until golden brown. Let muffins stand a few minutes; remove from pan. Cool 10 minutes. For optional glaze: Combine powdered sugar and milk; mix until smooth. Drizzle evenly over muffins.

Yield 12 muffins

Soft Pretzels

Terri Grimes, Indianapolis Indiana

These pretzels are very much reminiscent of the pretzels you get from venders in your local mall. You can make them plain, with salt, with sugar and cinnamon, or with Parmesan and garlic.

1-1/2 teaspoons active dry yeast

1/2 teaspoon brown sugar

1 dash salt

1 1/2 cups 110 degree water

4 cups bread flour

1 tablespoon baking soda

1/4 cup warm water

1 cup melted butter

Toppings (see Notes, below)

Combine yeast, brown sugar, salt and water. Allow to rest 5 minutes. Stir flour in mixture and knead 5 minutes. Place dough in lightly greased bowl, cover with a damp towel, and allow to rise 1 hour. Divide dough into 8-12 equal-size pieces; roll each piece into a rope; shape each rope into a pretzel. In a shallow dish, stir baking soda into warm water; brush mixture over pretzels. Lay coated pretzel onto a lightly greased cookie sheet. Put a topping on the pretzels if you desire. (See note below) Bake in a 550°F oven 8 minutes, or until golden. Brush melted butter onto hot pretzels.

Notes: For salted pretzels, sprinkle with kosher salt. For cinnamon-sugar pretzels, stir 2 tablespoons honey into the melted butter before brushing on pretzels, then sprinkle with a mixture of ½ cup sugar and 1 tsp. ground cinnamon. For Parmesan pretzels, sprinkle with a mixture of 1/4 cup grated Parmesan and 1-teaspoon garlic salt.

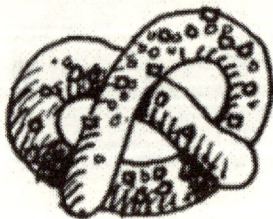

Sweet Potato Biscuits

Terri Grimes, Indianapolis Indiana

These biscuits are very popular on the Eastern Shore of Maryland where I am originally from. There was a popular restaurant there, The English Grill, which was known for their sweet potato biscuits. This recipe is tastes very much like theirs. As a shortcut, often I will merely take a can of sweet potatoes, drain them and mash, to use for the mashed sweet potatoes in this recipe.

1 cup all-purpose flour

2 tablespoons baking powder

½ teaspoon salt

2 tablespoons sugar

1/3 cup shortening

1 cup cooked mashed sweet potatoes

2 tablespoons milk

Preheat oven to 400°F. Combine flour, baking powder, salt and sugar. Cut in shortening with a pastry cutter. Mix in sweet potatoes. Add milk and combine. Turn dough onto lightly floured surface. Pat to ½ inch thickness. Cut with biscuit cutter. Place on lightly greased baking sheet. Bake 10 minutes.

Yield 8 Biscuits

Zucchini Bread

Terri Grimes, Indianapolis Indiana

What do you do when your family runs, screaming, from the table when they see you pulling another zucchini casserole out of the oven in middle of zucchini season? Make Zucchini bread of course! This is wonderful served for breakfast. Or frost a loaf with cream cheese frosting for a tasty dessert.

3 cups shredded zucchini (3 medium)	*1 teaspoon salt*
1 2/3 cups sugar	*1 teaspoon ground cinnamon*
2 teaspoons vanilla	*1/2 teaspoon ground cloves*
4 large eggs	*1/2 teaspoon baking powder*
3 cups all-purpose flour	*1/2 cup coarsely chopped nuts*

Preheat oven to 350°F. Grease bottoms of 2 loaf pans. Mix zucchini, sugar, oil, vanilla and eggs in large bowl. Stir in remaining ingredients. Pour into pans. Bake 8-inch loaves 50 to 60 minutes or until toothpick inserted in center comes out clean. Cool 10 minutes in pans. Remove from pans. Cool completely before slicing.

Yield 2 loaves

Cakes

CAKE

Angel Food Cake

Applesauce Cake

Banana Cream Cheesecake

Black Bottom Cupcakes

Cherry Cheesecake

Chocolate Chip Cheesecake

Christmas Cheesecake

Coconut Cupcakes

Cola Cake

Cola Icing

Deep Dark Chocolate Cake

Dirt Cake

Great Chocolate Cake

Greg's Yellow Cake

Hot Fudge Cake

Hot Milk Cake

Key Lime Cheesecake

Magnolia Bakery Chocolate cupcakes

Magnolia Bakery Vanilla cupcake

Oreo Cheesecake

Pistachio Cake

Pumpkin Cheesecake

Tomato Soup Cake

Vanilla Wafer Cake

Worlds Best Pound Cake

Yum Yum Cake

FROSTING

Coconut Frosting

Cream Cheese Frosting

Dark Chocolate Frosting

One Bowl Chocolate Buttercream Frosting

Seven Minute Frosting

Sour Cream Frosting

Vanilla Buttercream Frosting

Angel Food Cake

Terri Grimes, Indianapolis Indiana

Feathery light, deliciously sweet, angel food cake is one of those treats that can stand on its own. It's even better when covered with fresh berries or drizzled with chocolate syrup. Enjoy!

1 ½ cups cake flour, sifted

12 egg whites

1 ¼ teaspoon cream of tartar

¼ teaspoon salt

1 teaspoon vanilla extract

¼ teaspoon almond extract

1 1/3 cups sugar

Preheat oven to 375°F. For this recipe, you really need to sift the flour several times for a truly light, fluffy cake. After sifting flour, set aside. In a large bowl beat egg whites, cream of tartar, salt and extracts at high speed with an electric mixer until soft peaks form; this will take about 4 to 5 minutes. Gradually add sugar, 1/3 cup at a time, beating until blended after each addition. Fold in flour. Pour batter into an ungreased 10-inch tube pan. Bake 35 minutes. Invert pan on a wire rack, and let stand about 1 hour or until cake is completely cool. Run a knife around cake to loosen edges.

Applesauce Cake

Marion Grimes, Berlin Maryland

This was my husband's favorite cake. He passed away many years ago but every time I smell an Applesauce cake I still think of him.

1 cup butter

2 cups sugar

2 eggs

2 cups applesauce

4 cups all-purpose flour

2 teaspoons baking soda

2 teaspoons cinnamon

¾ teaspoon nutmeg

½ teaspoon ground cloves (optional)

¼ teaspoon allspice

Dash salt

2 cups raisins

1 cup nuts (I prefer walnuts)

Preheat oven to 325°F. Grease and flour a tube or bundt pan. Cream butter and sugar until light and fluffy. Add eggs, one at a time, beating well after each addition. Mix in applesauce. Sift dry ingredients together. Add dry ingredients to the butter mixture, a little at a time, beating well after each addition. Fold in raisins and nuts. Pour batter into prepared tube or bundt pan. Bake 1-½ hours or until toothpick inserted in center comes out clean. Check cake after 1 hour to make sure it doesn't burn.

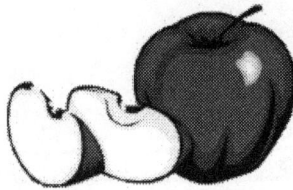

Banana Cream Cheesecake

Terri Grimes, Indianapolis Indiana

This is like a popular cheesecake restaurants, only better I think. And you don't have to stand in line to get it.

20 vanilla cream sandwich cookies, crushed into crumbs

1/4 cup melted butter

2 pounds cream cheese, softened

2/3 cup granulated sugar

2 tablespoons cornstarch

3 eggs

3/4 cup mashed ripe bananas

1/2 cup heavy whipping cream

2 teaspoons vanilla extract

Preheat oven to 350°F. Combine butter and cookie crumbs; press evenly into the bottom of a greased 10" springform pan; refrigerate. Beat cream cheese with an electric mixer until light and fluffy. Beat in sugar and cornstarch, then eggs, then bananas, whipping cream, and vanilla. Pour mixture over prepared crust. Place pan on a cookie sheet and bake in a 350 degree oven for 15 minutes. Reduce oven temperature to 200 degrees and bake an additional 75 minutes, or until center is almost set. Allow to cool completely, then refrigerate, uncovered, for at least 6 hours.

Black Bottom Cupcakes

Terri Grimes, Indianapolis Indiana

When Greg and I lived in Wisconsin a friend made these awesome cupcakes. They were so chocolaty and yummy I had to have the recipe. They have been one of our favorites ever since.

1 ½ cups flour

1 cup sugar

¼ cup cocoa

1 teaspoon baking soda

½ teaspoon salt

1 cup water

½ cup vegetable oil

1 tablespoon vinegar (I use apple cider vinegar)

1 teaspoon vanilla

One 8-ounce package cream cheese, softened

1 egg, beaten

1/3 cup sugar

One 6-ounce package semi-sweet chocolate chips

Preheat oven to 350°F. Combine flour, 1 cup sugar, cocoa, baking soda and salt in a mixing bowl. Whisk in water, oil, vinegar and vanilla until well combined. Pour batter into paper lined muffin cups, 2/3 full. Meanwhile in small bowl combine cream cheese, egg, and 1/3 cup sugar. Beat until smooth and creamy. Fold in chocolate chips. Place a heaping tablespoon-full of cream cheese mixture on top of each cupcake in the center of the batter. Bake 25 minutes.

Yields 24 cupcakes

Cherry Cheesecake

Julie Cameron, Des Moines Iowa

Cooking spray

¾ cup graham cracker crumbs

2 tablespoons sugar

2 tablespoons reduced-calorie stick margarine, melted

2/3 cup sugar

1/3 cup all-purpose flour

1 tablespoon cornstarch

1 teaspoon vanilla extract

One 8-ounce package 1/3-less-fat cream cheese (Neufchatel), softened

One 8-ounce package fat-free cream cheese, softened

2 large eggs

½ cup fat-free milk

1/3 cup fat-free sour cream

3 large egg whites

¼ cup sugar

One 20-ounce can light cherry pie filling

Preheat oven to 300°F. Coat a 9-inch springform pan with cooking spray. Combine crumbs, 2 tablespoons sugar, and margarine. Firmly press crumb mixture into bottom and 2 inches up sides of pan. Combine 2/3 cup sugar, flour, and next 5 ingredients (flour through eggs) in a large bowl; beat at high speed of a mixer until smooth. Add milk and sour cream to cheese mixture; beat until smooth. Beat egg whites (at room temperature) at high speed of a mixer until soft peaks form. Gradually add 1/4 cup sugar, 1 tablespoon at a time, beating until stiff peaks form using clean, dry beaters. Gently fold egg white mixture into cheese mixture. Pour into prepared pan. Bake 55 minutes or until almost set. Remove from oven and cool completely on a wire rack; cover and chill 8 hours. Top with pie filling.

Serves 12

Chocolate Chip Cheesecake

Terri Grimes, Indianapolis Indiana

Here's a delicious chocolate chip cheesecake with a chocolate wafer cookie crumb crust. As with most cheesecakes, make sure you make it the day before you plan to eat it as it needs quite a bit of time to chill. I have used everything from Oreo's to chocolate graham crackers for the crushed cookie crumbs in this recipe. All work really well.

1 1/4 cups chocolate wafer cookie crumbs

1/3 cup melted butter or margarine

24 ozs cream cheese, softened

3/4 cup sugar

2 eggs

2 teaspoons vanilla extract

1 1/3 cups miniature semisweet chocolate chips, divided

1/2 cup whipping cream

Combine chocolate cookie crumbs and butter, stirring well. Firmly press mixture evenly over the bottom of a 9-inch springform pan. Bake at 350°F for 5 minutes. Beat cream cheese at high speed of an electric hand-held mixer until light and fluffy; gradually add sugar, beating well. Add eggs, one at a time, beating after each addition. Stir in vanilla and 2/3 cup chocolate chips. Pour mixture into crust. Bake at 350°F for 40 minutes; turn oven off and leave oven door ajar. Leave cheesecake in the oven for 30 minutes. Remove from oven and let cool a on a wire rack. Cover cheesecake, refrigerate, and chill 8 hours. Melt remaining 2/3-cup chocolate chips in top of double boiler; gradually stir in whipping cream. Stir over low heat until thickened and smooth. Remove from heat and spread over cheesecake. Chill thoroughly.

Christmas Cheesecake

Barbara Dahan, Berlin Maryland

Zwieback is a teething biscuit and normally found on the baby food aisle of your supermarket. Every Christmas I make this cheesecake for my family. And every Christmas at least one member of my family will recant the tale of the year I stayed up until 2am on Christmas Eve making this cheesecake. It's not Christmas without this cheesecake and the story!

One 6-ounce package Zwieback	*1 cup sugar (for filling)*
1 cup Sugar (for crust)	*Three 8-ounce packages cream cheese*
1 teaspoon cinnamon	*½ pint whipping cream*
4 tablespoons butter, melted	*1 ½ teaspoons flour*
3 large eggs	*1 teaspoon vanilla*

Preheat oven to 250°F. Crush zwieback and roll to fine crumbs. Combine crumbs with 1 cup sugar and cinnamon. Reserve 3 tablespoons of crumb mixture for topping. Add melted butter to remaining crumb mixture, mixing until well blended. Press onto bottom and sides of 9-inch springform pan. To make filling, soften cream cheese and separate eggs. Place egg whites in fridge to chill. In large bowl beat 1 package softened cream cheese. Add 1 cup sugar, mixing well. Add egg yolks and 2nd package of cream cheese mixing until creamy. Add whipping cream slowly. Beat in 3rd package of cream cheese. Add flour and vanilla. Beat thoroughly until well blended and smooth. In separate bowl whip egg whites until stiff. Fold into cheese mixture. Turn into chilled Zwieback Crumb Crust and sprinkle top of cake with reserved crumbs. Bake 2 hours. Let cake cool completely in pan. When cool refrigerate.

Coconut Cupcakes

Terri Grimes, Indianapolis Indiana

After a trip to Los Angeles, where I was fortunate enough to eat several cupcakes from a bakery in Beverly Hills that caters to the stars, I was struck with a serious case of cupcake addiction. I have tried several cupcake recipes and after making a few variations to this one I have to say this one rivals the cupcakes I ate in Beverly Hills. Yes, it's that good!

¾ pound (3 sticks) unsalted butter, room temperature

2 cups sugar

6 large eggs, room temperature

1 ½ teaspoons vanilla extract

1 teaspoon almond extract

3 cups all-purpose flour

1 teaspoon baking powder

½ teaspoon baking soda

½ teaspoon salt

1 cup buttermilk

14-ounces sweetened shredded coconut

Preheat the oven to 325°F. In large mixing bowl cream butter and sugar until light and fluffy (3-5 minutes). Add eggs, 1 at a time, beating after each addition. Add the vanilla and almond extracts and mix well. In separate bowl, sift together flour, baking powder, baking soda, and salt. Alternately add dry ingredients and buttermilk to the batter. Mix until combined. Fold half of the coconut into the batter. Line muffin tins with paper liners. Fill each liner to the top with batter. Bake for 25 to 35 minutes, until the tops are brown and a toothpick comes out clean. Allow to cool in the pan for 15 minutes. Remove to a baking rack and cool completely. Frost with coconut frosting.

This recipe makes 18 totally awesome cupcakes.

Cola Cake

Cindy Newsom, Walker Louisiana

2 cups Flour

2 cups Sugar

1 cup Coca-Cola (Regular NOT diet)

6 tablespoons Cocoa (level tablespoons)

1 cup butter

2 eggs, well beaten

1 tablespoon baking soda

½ cup buttermilk

1½ cups miniature marshmallows

Preheat oven to 350°F. Grease and flour a 9 x 13" pan. In medium bowl combine flour and sugar. Bring cola, cocoa and butter to a boil; then add to flour mixture. Combine eggs, baking soda and buttermilk. Then add to flour mixture, beating well. Fold in marshmallows. Bake 30 - 35 minutes or until toothpick inserted in center comes out clean.

Cola Icing

Cindy Newsom, Walker Louisiana

½ cup butter

3 tablespoons cocoa (level tablespoons)

½ cup Coca-cola (regular, NOT diet)

1 pound powdered sugar

1 cup chopped nuts (optional)

Melt butter in a small saucepan. Add cocoa and cola. Bring to a boil and let boil for 1 or 2 minutes. Pour over the powdered sugar and mix well. Add nuts. Pour frosting on Cola cake. Cool before serving.

Deep Dark Chocolate Cake

Greg Grimes, Indianapolis Indiana

1 ¾ cup all-purpose flour	2 eggs
2 cups sugar	1 cup milk
¾ cup cocoa	½ cup vegetable oil
1 ½ teaspoons baking soda	2 teaspoons vanilla
1 teaspoon salt	1 cup boiling water

Preheat oven to 350°F. Combine dry ingredients in a medium bowl. Add eggs, milk, oil and vanilla, beating well. Beat two minutes. Stir in boiling water, mixing well. Pour batter into two greased and floured 9-inch cake pans. Bake 35 minutes. When cool frost cake with One-bowl Chocolate Buttercream frosting or Dark Chocolate frosting.

Serves 8

Dirt Cake

Cindy Newsom, Walker Louisiana

1 package Oreo cookies (large package)	One 3-ounce package French Vanilla instant pudding
4 tablespoons (½ stick) butter	2 ¼ cup Milk
8-ounces cream cheese	12-ounces Cool Whip, thawed
¼ cup Powdered sugar	1 package Gummy Worms (optional)

Crush cookies in food processor or chopper and set aside. Cookies should be crushed to the consistency of dirt. Mix margarine, cream cheese and powdered sugar until creamy. In another bowl, mix pudding and milk until thick. Mix together with cream cheese mixture. Blend in the Cool Whip. In a lined flowerpot, add a layer of cookies, then pudding mixture. Continue alternating layers, ending with cookies. Push Gummy Worms into top layer, as if coming out of the "Dirt". Use a new gardening trowel for a serving piece. You can even add a fake plant in the "Dirt" for additional appeal.

Great Chocolate Cake

Sharon Lehrer, Roseville CA

I got this recipe from one of my church's ladies Christmas functions. When ever we go to my friend Carol's house during the holidays the only thing I can bring is this cake and my home made vanilla ice cream.

One 18 ¾-ounce package chocolate cake mix

One 6-ounce box of chocolate pudding mix (the kind you cook not instant)

6-ounce package semisweet chocolate chips

Preheat oven to 350°F. Follow the directions on the pudding box; make it as if you are making the pudding. When it starts to get thick turn off the heat and pour in the cake mix and the choc chips. Mix well. Pour into a greased and floured 13 x 9 pan. Bake 25 minutes. Cool before serving. I usually serve it with vanilla ice cream.

Variation: The kids' favorite way for me to make this is to use the chocolate cake mix, banana pudding and peanut butter chips. Both ways are great.

Greg's Yellow Cake

Greg Grimes, Indianapolis Indiana

For several years I would make this coconut cake on Christmas Eve for my family. I would frost it with coconut frosting and sprinkle additional coconut on top. It's also excellent with a chocolate frosting.

2 1/2 cups sifted cake flour	2/3 cup shortening
1 2/3 cups sugar	3 eggs
3 1/2 teaspoons baking powder	1/2 cup milk
1 teaspoon salt	1 teaspoon vanilla
3/4 cup milk	

Preheat oven to 350°F. In mixing bowl, combine the cake flour, sugar, baking powder, and salt. Add the 3/4 cup milk and the Crisco. Beat with electric mixer at medium speed for 2 minutes, or beat vigorously by hand for 300 strokes. Add eggs, the 1/2 cup milk, and the vanilla. Beat 2 minutes more or 300 strokes. Pour batter into 2 greased and floured 9 x 1-1/2-inch round layer pans. Bake at 350°F for 35 to 40 minutes or till cake tests done. Cool 15 minutes; remove cake from pans. Or, bake 35 to 40 minutes in a 13 x 9 x 2-inch baking pan. Frost when cool.

Hot Fudge Cake

Terri Grimes, Indianapolis Indiana

This yummy cakes oozes decadent hot fudge when you cut into it. Delicious served with vanilla ice cream.

1 cup all-purpose flour	*½ cup milk*
¾ cup sugar	*2 tablespoons vegetable oil*
6 tablespoons cocoa	*1 teaspoon vanilla*
2 teaspoons baking powder	*1 cup packed brown sugar*
¼ teaspoon salt	*1 ¾ cup boiling water*

In mixing bowl combine flour, sugar, 2 tablespoons cocoa, baking powder and salt. Stir in milk, oil and vanilla. Beat until smooth. Spread in ungreased 9-inch square baking dish. Combine brown sugar and remaining cocoa. Sprinkle evenly over cake batter. Pour boiling water evenly over top cake. Do not stir! Bake 35 minutes. Serve while warm.

Serves 6

Hot Milk Cake

Mabel Baker, Salisbury Maryland

Note from Terri: Mabel is no longer with us but every time I make this cake I think about her. After tasting this cake in 1980 I begged her for the recipe. Classic hot-milk cakes date at least to the Great Depression and are light, buttery, and golden. The hot milk begins to poach the eggs. So the finished cake tastes rich and almost feathery. Mabel's version was the best one I have tasted. I think you will enjoy it too!

4 eggs	*Pinch of salt*
2 cups sugar	*2 teaspoons vanilla extract*
2 cups all-purpose flour	*1 cup milk*
2 teaspoons baking powder	*1/4 pound (1 stick) butter*

Preheat oven to 350°F. Grease and flour 13x9 pan. In large mixing bowl beat eggs until light. Gradually add sugar and beat until light and fluffy. In separate bowl, combine flour, baking powder and salt. Add to egg mixture and fold together. Heat milk and butter in a saucepan until hot. Don't boil! Add hot milk mixture to cake batter and stir until combined. Add vanilla and stir until vanilla is incorporated into batter. Pour batter into prepared pan. Bake 40 - 50 minutes, or just until a toothpick inserted in the center comes out clean. When cool dust with powdered sugar. Makes one 13x9 cake or two 8 or 9 inch layers.

Key Lime Cheesecake

Terri Grimes, Indianapolis Indiana

2 cups graham cracker crumbs

1/4 cup sugar

1/2 cup butter, melted

Three 8-ounce packages cream cheese

1 1/4 cups sugar

6 large eggs, separated

One 8-ounce carton sour cream

1 ½ teaspoon grated lime rind

½ cup Key lime juice

Combine first 3 ingredients in a small bowl, stirring well. Firmly press mixture in bottom and 1" up sides of a buttered 9" springform pan. Bake crust at 350°F for 8 minutes; cool in pan on a wire rack. Meanwhile beat cream cheese at medium speed with an electric mixer until creamy; gradually add 1 1/4 cups sugar. Add egg yolks one at a time, beating after each addition. Stir in sour cream, lime rind, and Key lime juice. Beat egg whites at high speed until stiff peaks form; fold into cream cheese mixture. Pour batter into prepared crust, and bake at 350°F for 1 hour and 5 minutes; turn oven off. Partially open oven door; let cheesecake cool in oven 15 minutes. Remove from oven, and immediately run a knife around edge of pan to release sides. Cool completely in pan on a wire rack; cover and chill 8 hours.

Magnolia Bakery Chocolate Cupcakes

Magnolia Bakery, New York, New York

This is from New York's most famous cupcake bakery. I like to ice these with dark Chocolate Frosting or Chocolate Buttercream.

2 cups all-purpose flour

1 teaspoon baking soda

1 cup (2 sticks) unsalted butter, softened

1 cup granulated sugar

1 cup firmly packed light brown sugar

4 large eggs, at room temperature

6-ounces unsweetened chocolate, melted

1 cup buttermilk

1 teaspoon vanilla extract

Preheat oven to 350°F. Line two 12-cup muffin tins with cupcake papers. In a small bowl, sift together flour and baking soda. Set aside. In a large bowl cream butter until smooth. Add the sugars and beat until fluffy, about 3 minutes. Add the eggs, one at a time, beating well after each addition. Add the chocolate, mixing until well incorporated. Add the dry ingredients in three parts, alternating with the buttermilk and vanilla. With each addition, beat until the ingredients are incorporated, but do not over beat. Using a rubber spatula, scrape down the batter in the bowl to make sure the ingredients are well blended and the batter is smooth. Carefully spoon the batter into the cupcake liners, filling them about three-quarters full. Bake for 20–25 minutes, or until a toothpick inserted in center of the cupcake comes out clean. Cool the cupcakes completely before icing.

Variation: If you would like to make a layer cake instead of cupcakes, divide the batter between two 9-inch round cake pans and bake the layers for 30–40 minutes.

Yield 24 cupcakes

Magnolia Bakery Vanilla Cupcakes

Magnolia Bakery, New York, New York

This is the most popular cupcake at New York's most famous cupcake bakery. The most popular icing to pair this cupcake with is the Vanilla Buttercream icing tinted pink.

1 1/2 cups self-rising flour

1 1/4 cups all-purpose flour

1 cup (2 sticks) unsalted butter, softened

2 cups sugar

4 large eggs, at room temperature

1 cup milk

1 teaspoon vanilla extract

Preheat oven to 350°F. Line two 12-cup muffin tins with cupcake papers. In a small bowl, combine the flours. Set aside. In a large bowl, on the medium speed of an electric mixer, cream the butter until smooth. Add the sugar gradually and beat until fluffy, about 3 minutes. Add the eggs, one at a time, beating well after each addition. Add the dry ingredients in three parts, alternating with the milk and vanilla. With each addition, beat until the ingredients are incorporated but do not over beat. Using a rubber spatula, scrape down the batter in the bowl to make sure the ingredients are well blended. Carefully spoon the batter into the cupcake liners, filling them about three-quarters full. Bake for 20–25 minutes, or until a cake tester inserted in the center of the cupcake comes out clean. Cool the cupcakes completely before icing.

Yield 24 cupcakes

Oreo Cheesecake

Terri Grimes, Indianapolis Indiana

2 tablespoons melted butter

1 1/2 cups Oreo cookie crumbs

Three 8-ounce packages cream cheese, softened

1 cup granulated sugar

5 eggs, room temperature

1 cup sour cream, room temperature

1/4 cup all-purpose flour

2 teaspoons vanilla extract

1/4 teaspoon salt

15 Oreo cookies, coarsely chopped, divided

Preheat oven to 325°F. Combine butter and cookie crumbs; press evenly into the bottom of a greased 10" springform pan; refrigerate. Beat cream cheese with an electric mixer until light and fluffy. Beat in sugar, then eggs. Stir in sour cream, flour, vanilla, and salt. Gently stir in 5 chopped cookies. Pour mixture into springform pan; top with remaining chopped cookies. Bake 75 minutes. Turn off oven, prop door open several inches, and allow cake rest in oven for 1 hour. Refrigerate.

Pistachio Cake

Terri Grimes, Indianapolis Indiana

Note: Make sure the cake mix is not the kind that has the pudding in it. You want a plain yellow cake mix for this recipe. If you don't like pistachio you can always substitute the pistachio pudding for another variety. Give the pistachio a try though, it's really good!

Two 3-ounce packages instant pistachio pudding

One 18-ounce package yellow cake mix

4 eggs

1 cup club soda

½ cup oil

1 cup chopped walnuts

¾ cup milk

½ pint heavy cream

Few drops green food coloring (optional)

Preheat oven to 350°F. Mix 1 package instant pudding mix with yellow cake mix. Add in eggs, club soda and oil, beating 4 minutes on medium speed. Fold in walnuts. Pour batter in a greased and floured 10-inch bundt pan. Bake 30 minutes or until cake tester or toothpick comes out clean when inserted in center of cake. After cake cools make icing by combining remaining package of instant pudding with milk, heavy cream and food coloring. Beat until peaks form. Spread on cooled cake.

Serves 10

Pumpkin Cheesecake

Terri Grimes, Indianapolis Indiana

3/4 cup graham cracker crumbs	24-ounces cream cheese, softened
1 cup chopped pecans	1/2 cup sugar
1/2 cup sugar	3 tablespoons whipping cream
1/4 cup melted butter	1 tablespoon cornstarch
One 15-ounce can pumpkin	1 tablespoon vanilla extract
3 eggs	1 tablespoon bourbon
2 teaspoons cinnamon	**Topping**
3/4 teaspoon nutmeg	2 cups sour cream
1/2 teaspoon ground ginger	2 tablespoons sugar
1/2 teaspoon salt	1 ½ tablespoons bourbon
1/2 cup packed light brown sugar	Pecan halves

Prepare crust. Butter a 9-inch springform pan. Combine crumbs, pecans, sugar in a bowl. Stir in melted butter. Press mixture over bottom and 1/2 inch up side of pan. Chill, covered, in the refrigerator for about 1 hour. Preheat oven to 350°F. Whisk together pumpkin, eggs, cinnamon, nutmeg, ginger, salt, and brown sugar in bowl. Cut cream cheese into chunks and cream together with the sugar in bowl of electric mixer. Beat in cream, cornstarch, vanilla, bourbon, and pumpkin mixture until smooth. Pour into crust. Bake on the middle rack of oven for 50-55 minutes or until the center is set. Let cook in the pan on a wire rack for 10 minutes. For topping, whisk the sour cream, sugar and bourbon in a bowl. Spread over cheesecake. Bake for 5 minutes. Let cool in pan on wire rack. Cover and chill overnight before serving. Remove sides and decorate with pecan halves.

Serves 10

Tomato Soup Cake

Terri Grimes, Indianapolis Indiana

I know, I know - tomato soup is an odd ingredient for a cake. But try it! It tastes similar to a spice cake and is so yummy. People can't taste tomato soup in the cake even when you tell them it is there.

2 1/4 cups cake flour	1/2 teaspoon ground cloves
1 1/3 cup sugar	One 10 ¾-ounce can tomato soup
4 teaspoons baking powder	1/2 cup shortening
1 teaspoons baking soda	2 eggs
1 1/2 teaspoon allspice	1/4 cup water
1 teaspoon cinnamon	

Preheat oven to 350°F. Generously grease and flour two round layer pans, 8 or 9 inches or 13 x 9 pan. Measure dry ingredients into large bowl. Add soup and shortening. Beat at low to medium speed for 2 minutes (300 strokes with a spoon) scraping sides and bottom of bowl constantly. Add eggs and water. Beat 2 minutes more, scraping bowl frequently. Pour into pans. Bake 35 or 40 minutes. Let stand in pans 10 minutes; remove and cool on rack. Frost with cream cheese frosting when cake is cool.

VARIATION: Nut or Raisin: After mixing, fold in 1 cup chopped nuts or raisins (or both). Bake 35 to 40 minutes.

Vanilla Wafer Cake

Terri Grimes, Indianapolis Indiana

1 cup (2 sticks) butter, softened

2 cups sugar

2 cups chopped pecans

5 eggs, at room temperature

One 3 ½-ounce can coconut flakes

12-ounces vanilla wafer cookies, crushed

1/2 cup Sweetened Condensed milk

Preheat oven to 325°F. Grease and flour a tube cake pan. Cream butter and sugar. Add eggs one at a time beating after each addition. Add half of wafers crushed fine. Mix in coconut, nuts, milk, and lastly the remaining crushed wafers. Pour batter into tube pan. Bake 1 hour or until toothpick inserted in center is clean. Leave cake in pan 10 minutes to cool; turn out onto cake plate.

Worlds Best Pound Cake

Terri Grimes, Indianapolis Indiana

This recipe originally called for Imperial margarine instead of butter. While it made a great pound cake using Imperial margarine, it makes an astounding pound cake using butter. And yes, there is no baking powder in this recipe.

1 pound unsalted butter

6 eggs

1 pound confectioners sugar

3 cups cake flour

2 teaspoons vanilla

Preheat oven to 325°F. Cream butter and sugar. Add eggs one at a time, beating well after each addition. Add flour and mix well. Add vanilla before, during, and after adding the flour. Pour batter into greased and floured bundt cake pan. Bake 1 to 1 ½ hours. Begin watching the cake at 1 hour. The cake is done when a toothpick inserted into the center comes out clean. Cake should be cracked on top and golden brown. Let cake cool in pan for 5 minutes on a cake rack. Loosen the sides with a knife. Gently remove the cake from the pan while still warm.

Yum Yum Cake

Cindy Newsom, Walker Louisiana

One 18 ½-ounce yellow cake mix, (Pudding in the mix)

Two 3.4-ounce packages instant vanilla pudding

8-ounces Cool Whip, thawed

½ cup walnuts (or pecans)

One 15-ounce can crushed pineapple

Prepare cake as directed on back of box (13 x 9 cake pan). Bake as directed and let cool. Spread Pineapple on top of cake. Prepare both packages of vanilla pudding as directed on package. Pour pudding over top of entire cake. Spread thawed cool whip on top of cake. Sprinkle walnuts or pecans lightly on top. Refrigerate at least one hour prior to serving. Keep any leftovers in refrigerator.

Coconut Frosting

Terri Grimes, Indianapolis Indiana

This recipe makes the creamiest, melt in your mouth frosting. Frost coconut cupcakes, coconut cake or even a custard pie with this recipe.

1 lb cream cheese, room temperature

½ teaspoon almond extract

¾ lb (3 sticks) unsalted butter, room temperature

1 ½ lbs confectioners' sugar, sifted

7-ounces sweetened shredded coconut

1 teaspoon vanilla extract

In mixing bowl cream together cream cheese, butter, vanilla and almond extracts until fluffy. Gradually beat in confectioners' sugar and mix until smooth and fluffy. Frost cupcakes or cake and sprinkle top liberally with coconut.

Cream Cheese Frosting

Terri Grimes, Indianapolis Indiana

I use this yummy frosting to top my tomato soup cake. It's great on applesauce cakes and chocolate cakes as well.

8-ounces cream cheese, softened

¼ cup butter

2 cups confectioners' sugar, sifted

1 teaspoon vanilla

Beat cream cheese and butter until fluffy. Add in sugar and vanilla. Beat well until blended and smooth. This should be enough to fill and frost a two-layer 8-inch cake or 24 cupcakes.

Dark Chocolate Frosting

Terri Grimes, Indianapolis Indiana

This delicious dark chocolate frosting will make your cupcakes stand out. This frosting is good enough to eat on it's own. It's seriously good!

5-ounces bittersweet chocolate, chopped

½ pound (2 sticks) unsalted butter, at room temp

¾ lb powdered sugar

1/8 teaspoon salt

1 teaspoon vanilla extract

¼ cup sour cream

Melt and cool chocolate (until just slightly warm). Beat butter until light and fluffy. With mixer on low speed, gradually add powdered sugar. Add salt, vanilla and sour cream and mix until very smooth. Add chocolate and mix until just incorporated. Don't over-whip and add too much air into the frosting. The consistency should be rich and dense, like ice cream.

Frosts 2 dozen cupcakes or one layer cake.

One Bowl Chocolate Buttercream Frosting

Greg Grimes, Indianapolis Indiana

This is the frosting I use for my famous Dark Chocolate Cake.

½ cup cocoa

2 cups powdered sugar

6 tablespoons butter, softened

4 tablespoons milk or water

1 teaspoon vanilla extract

In small bowl, stir together cocoa and sugar. In medium bowl, cream butter until light and fluffy. Add small amounts of cocoa mixture alternately small amounts of with milk, beating to spreading consistency. Blend in vanilla.

Yields 2 cups frosting

Seven Minute Frosting

Terri Grimes, Indianapolis Indiana

1 ½ cup sugar

¼ teaspoon cream of tartar

1/8 teaspoon salt

1/3 cup water

2 egg whites

1 ½ teaspoons vanilla

Place sugar, cream of tartar, salt, water, and egg whites in the top of a double boiler. Beat with a handheld electric mixer for 1 minute. Place pan over boiling water, being sure that boiling water does not touch the bottom of the top pan. (If this happens, it could cause your frosting to become grainy). Beat constantly on high speed with electric mixer for 7 minutes. Beat in vanilla. This recipe frosts 1 layer cake or approximately 8 to 12 cup cakes.

Sour Cream Frosting

Terri Grimes, Indianapolis Indiana

1/3 cup butter, softened

3 cups powdered sugar

½ cup sour cream

2 teaspoons vanilla

Cream butter and powdered sugar until light and fluffy. Mix in sour cream and vanilla. Beat until smooth and spreadable. Frosts one 13x9 inch cake or one 8-or 9-inch two layer cake.

Vanilla Buttercream Frosting

Terri Grimes, Indianapolis Indiana

4 ½ cups powdered sugar

½ cup butter, softened

2 teaspoons vanilla

2 to 3 tablespoons milk

Cream sugar and butter in medium bowl. Stir in vanilla and milk. Beat until smooth and spreadable. Frosts one 13x9-inch cake or fills and frosts one 8-or 9-inch two-layer cake.

Pies

Apple Crumb Pie

Berry Apple Pie

Cherry Berry Pie

Classic Pecan Pie

Fluffy Key Lime Pie

Fried Apple Pies

Fudge Crostada

Hoosier Sugar Cream Pie

Lemon Cheesecake Pie

Lemon Icebox Pie

Lemon Pie

Mock Apple Pie

Peach Cobbler

Pumpkin Pie

Sweet Potato Pie

Apple Crumb Pie

Terri Grimes, Indianapolis Indiana

This is a nice twist on a classic pie. And by using the canned apple filling and the pre-made graham cracker crust, it is so easy!

One 21-ounce can apple pie filling

½ cup flour

¼ cup sugar

1 ½ teaspoon cinnamon

¼ cup (1/2 stick) cold butter

¾ cup chopped pecans

1 tablespoon powdered sugar

1 graham cracker pie crust

Preheat oven to 375°F. Spoon apple pie filling in crust. In bowl combine flour, sugar and cinnamon. Cut in butter with a pastry cutter until mixture resembles coarse crumbs. Add in chopped pecans and stir well. Sprinkle mixture over pie filling. Bake 25 minutes or until topping is golden brown.

Serves 8

Berry Apple Pie

Terri Grimes, Indianapolis Indiana

One 2-crust package refrigerated pie crusts

1 cup sugar

2 cups sliced, peeled apples

2 tablespoons butter, cut on small pieces

Preheat oven to 375°F. Place one pie crust in bottom of a 9-inch pie pan. In bowl combine sugar, tapioca, and cinnamon. Add blackberries and apple slices. Toss to coat. Let stand 15 minutes. Spoon filling into pastry. Dot with butter. Put top crust on pie. Seal edges of crusts and flute. Cut small hole in center of pie to allow steam to escape during baking. Lightly brush pie with beaten egg. Sprinkle 2 tablespoons of sugar evenly over pie. Cover edge of crust with foil strip to keep from over browning. Bake 25 minutes. Remove foil. Bake 20 – 25 minutes more or until the crust is golden. Cool completely before cutting.

Serves 8

Cherry Berry Pie

Terri Grimes, Indianapolis Indiana

This pie is the favorite of my eldest son, Andrew. I make it for him every Thanksgiving and Christmas. Each family member has a different favorite pie. They keep me busy making them all at holiday time.

One 2-crust package refrigerated pie crusts

2 cups frozen blueberries (do not thaw)

½ cup sugar

1 tablespoon all-purpose flour

One 21-ounce can cherry pie filling

1 egg, beaten

2 tablespoons sugar

Preheat oven to 400°F. Place one pie crust in bottom of a 9-inch pie pan. In large bowl combine frozen blueberries with ½ cup sugar and flour. Fold in cherry pie filling. Pour on pastry. Top with second crust. Seal edges of crusts and flute. Cut small hole in center of pie to allow steam to escape during baking. Lightly brush pie with beaten egg. Sprinkle 2 tablespoons of sugar evenly over pie. Bake 40 – 45 minutes or until crust is golden brown. Allow to cool completely before cutting.

Serves 8

Classic Pecan Pie

Terri Grimes, Indianapolis Indiana

This is my husband's favorite holiday pie. In my house everyone has a different favorite pie and at the holidays I make everyone's favorite.

3 eggs, slightly beaten

1 cup sugar

1 cup light corn syrup

2 tablespoons butter, melted

1 teaspoon vanilla

1 1/4 cup pecans

1 unbaked 9-inch pie shell (deep-dish)

Preheat oven to 350°F. In medium bowl with fork beat eggs slightly. Add sugar, corn syrup, margarine and vanilla; stir until blended. Stir in pecans. Pour into piecrust. Bake 50 to 55 minutes or until knife inserted halfway between center and edge comes out clean. Cool on wire rack.

Fluffy Key Lime Pie

Terri Grimes, Indianapolis Indiana

2 cups cold milk

Two 3-ounce packages Vanilla instant pudding

2 teaspoons lime zest

8-ounces Cool Whip, thawed

1 graham cracker pie crust

8 thin lime slices for garnish (optional)

In large bowl beat milk, instant pudding and lime zest with electric mixer on low or wire whisk for one minute. Mixture will be thick. Fold in half of the Cool Whip. Refrigerate at least 4 hours. Garnish with remaining whipped cream and lime slices.

Serves 8

Fried Apple Pies

Terri Grimes, Indianapolis Indiana

2 tablespoons butter

4 Granny Smith apples, peeled, cored and sliced

½ cup sugar

1 teaspoon lemon juice

One 10-ounce tube flaky biscuit dough

Heat a deep fryer to 350 degrees. Meanwhile, add butter to large sauté pan and melt. Add apples, sugar, cinnamon, and lemon juice. Cook over medium heat until the apples are soft, about 10 minutes. Remove from the heat and cool. Roll biscuits on lightly floured surface so each biscuit forms a 7 to 8-inch circle. Place 2 to 3 tablespoons of the filling on 1/2 of each circle. Brush the edges of the circle with water. Fold the circle over the filling to make a half-moon shapes. Seal by pressing the edges with the tines of a fork. Carefully add the pies to the oil, 1 at a time, and fry until golden brown, turning the pies as necessary for even browning, about 5 to 8 minutes. Drain on paper towels. Sprinkle with powdered sugar immediately.

Serves 8

Fudge Crostada

Terri Grimes, Indianapolis Indiana

This pie is the favorite of my daughter, Brooke. Instead of a cake at her birthday, she usually requests this pie. After tasting it you will understand why she loves it so.

One 2-crust package refrigerated pie crusts

8 tablespoons butter

2/3 cup sugar

1 cup finely ground almonds

1 egg

1 egg, separated

1 teaspoon vanilla

One 6-ounce package semi-sweet chocolate chips

Preheat oven to 425°F. Put one piecrust in the bottom of a 9-inch pie pan. In small saucepan melt chocolate chips and 2 tablespoons butter; stirring constantly until smooth and chocolate is melted. In mixing bowl beat remaining 6 tablespoons butter with sugar until light and fluffy. Add almonds, 1 whole egg and egg yolk. Slowly add melted chocolate, blending well. Stir in vanilla. Spread chocolate mixture over pie crust in pie pan. With the remaining pie crust make a lattice top for the pie. Brush lattice top with beaten egg white. Bake at 425°F 10 minutes. Reduce heat to 350°F and bake an additional 30 minutes. Serve when cool. I like to top each serving with a dollop of whipped cream and fresh raspberries.

Serves 8

Hoosier Sugar Cream Pie

Terri Grimes, Indianapolis Indiana

I never heard of a Sugar Cream pie until we moved to Indiana and became Hoosiers in the mid-90's. This pie is a Hoosier staple. Definitely a comfort food.

1 1/3 cups sugar

½ cup all-purpose flour

1 cup heavy whipping cream

¾ cup milk

1 unbaked 9" pie shell

2 tablespoons butter, cut into small pieces

1 pinch nutmeg

Preheat oven to 425 degrees. Combine sugar, flour, cream, and milk in a mixing bowl. Pour into pie shell. Dot butter bits all around top of pie. Sprinkle with nutmeg. Bake for approximately 10 minutes, and then reduce the heat to 350 degrees and cook for approximately 30 more minutes. Cool to room temperature and then refrigerate until chilled. Serve chilled.

Serves 6 to 8

Lemon Cheesecake Pie

Terri Grimes, Indianapolis Indiana

Two 8-ounce packages cream cheese, softened

½ cup sugar

½ cup sour cream

1 tablespoon fresh lemon juice

1 teaspoon lemon zest

2 eggs

1 graham cracker pie crust

Preheat oven to 375°F. In medium bowl beat cream cheese until creamy. Add sugar, beating until well blended. Add sour cream, lemon juice and zest, beating well. Add eggs, one at a time, beating well after each addition. Pour mixture into pie shell. Bake 35 to 40 minutes or until center is almost set. After cooling refrigerate at least 4 hours.

Serves 8

Lemon Icebox Pie

Helen Giddings, Laurel Maryland

Greg's Note: My grandmother, Helen Giddings, used to make this pie for special occasions along with every other cake, pie and dessert known to man. She would have rooms of food when she would cook a holiday meal. One entire room would be nothing but desserts. She was not one to write recipes down, but I loved this pie so much that she let me watch her make it and write down the steps. I wrote it on a paper napkin and unfortunately lost it. Terri tried to recreate the recipe but wasn't able to quite get it. I did a lot of pie tasting. After Terri's 5th pie attempt in as many days, my mother found the paper napkin. I can't tell you how happy that made Terri and I!

One 3-ounce package lemon jello

1 cup orange juice

2/3 cup sugar

1 teaspoon lemon zest

One 12-ounce can Pet evaporated milk, chilled

30 Vanilla wafers

In small saucepan bring jello, orange juice and sugar to a boil, stirring often. Pour in a bowl and refrigerate approximately 15 minutes or until mixture is slightly thickened. Meanwhile place vanilla wafers in the bottom and up the sides of a 9-inch pie pan. Set aside. In large bowl beat Pet evaporated milk on high speed until it peaks, approximately 5 to 10 minutes. Fold in jello mixture until combined. Pour filling into the cookie lined pie plate. Refrigerate several hours or until firm.

Serves **8**

Lemon Pie

Jennifer Macaire, Montchauvet France

75 grams melted (then cooled) butter	*2 eggs*
250 grams sugar	*One 9-inch pie crust*
2 lemons (bio - non treated)	

Preheat oven to 220°C. Grate the lemon zest and press the two lemons for their juice. In a bowl, beat the sugar and the eggs. Add the melted butter, the lemon juice and the zest. Mix. Pour this into piecrust and bake for 35 min.

Serves 8

Mock Apple Pie

Terri Grimes, Indianapolis Indiana

First published in 1863 in the Confederate Receipt Book, this recipe originally called for soda crackers. Over the years the recipe changed to Ritz crackers. Created for the home cook who couldn't afford fresh apples, this pie tastes exactly like apple pie. It's amazing but it even looks like apple pie.

Pastry for 2-crust 9-inch pie	*Grated peel of 1 lemon*
36 Ritz Crackers, coarsely broken	*2 tablespoons lemon juice*
2 cups sugar	*2 tablespoons butter or margarine*
2 teaspoons cream of tartar	*1/2 teaspoons ground cinnamon*

Preheat oven to 425°F. Roll out half the pastry and place in 9-inch pie plate. Place cracker crumbs in crust; set aside. Mix sugar and cream of tartar in saucepan. Stir in 1-3/4 cups water until well blended. Bring to boil then reduce heat to low; simmer 15 minutes. Add lemon peel and juice; cool. Pour syrup over cracker crumbs. Dot with butter; sprinkle with cinnamon. Top pie with remaining pastry. Trim; seal and flute edges. Slit top crust to allow steam to escape. Bake 30 to 35 minutes or until crust is golden. Cool completely.

Peach Cobbler

Terri Grimes, Indianapolis Indiana

This is the easiest, best tasting cobbler you'll ever make! You can use other fruits in place of the peaches and prepare in the same manner.

5 cups peeled and sliced fresh peaches

¼ pound (1 stick) butter, melted

1 cup flour

1 ½ cups sugar

2 teaspoons baking powder

¼ teaspoon salt

1 cup milk

½ teaspoon cinnamon

¼ teaspoon nutmeg

Preheat oven to 350°F. Butter and flour a 9x13 baking dish. In saucepan cook peaches, ½ cup sugar, cinnamon and nutmeg till peaches are soft. In medium bowl combine flour, remaining sugar, baking powder and salt. Whisk in milk until smooth. Pour melted butter into baking dish. Pour flour/milk mixture evenly over butter. Pour peaches evenly over batter. Bake 45 minutes.

Serves 6 to 8

Pumpkin Pie

Terri Grimes, Indianapolis Indiana

It's not a holiday without a Pumpkin Pie. Although I make 4 to 5 pies at Thanksgiving and Christmas, this is my granddaughter Jasmine's favorite pie. She is a whiz at whisking the ingredients together.

1 unbaked 9-inch pie shell (deep-dish)	*1/2 teaspoon ground ginger*
3/4 cup granulated sugar	*2 large eggs*
1 teaspoon ground cinnamon	*One 15-ounce can Pumpkin*
1/2 teaspoon salt	*One 12-ounce can Evaporated Milk*

Preheat oven to 425° F. Mix sugar, salt, cinnamon, ginger and cloves in small bowl. Meanwhile beat eggs in large bowl. Stir in pumpkin and sugar-spice mixture. Gradually stir in evaporated milk. Mix well. Pour into unbaked pie shell. BAKE for 15 minutes at 425°F. Reduce temperature to 350°F. Bake for an additional 40 to 50 minutes or until knife inserted near center comes out clean. Cool on wire rack for 2 hours before serving. I prefer serving with a dollop of homemade whipped cream on top. Refrigerate leftovers.

Makes 8 servings

Sweet Potato Pie

Lottie Smith, Salisbury Maryland

Terri's Note: Although this pie tastes similar to pumpkin pie Grandmom would make both Pumpkin and Sweet Potato pies at Thanksgiving and Christmas. My Aunt Geraldine was fond of this recipe also and once made my cousin Sharon and I both pies to take home. Unfortunately she forgot to test the sweet potato and as a result they were still slightly raw. It was the only Sweet Potato pie Sharon and I ever had that crunched when we ate it. It tasted good nonetheless.

1 cup mashed sweet potatoes

1 cup sugar

2 eggs

1 cup milk

1 ½ teaspoons vanilla

½ teaspoon nutmeg

2 tablespoons butter

Preheat oven to 350°F. Beat potatoes, sugar, eggs, milk, vanilla, nutmeg and butter until light and fluffy. Pour into 9-inch piecrust and bake 45 minutes. Let cool before serving.

Cookies

Cherry Mocha Balls
Chocolate Caramel Poppers
Chocolate Chai Latte Cookies
Chocolate Pecan Pralines
Church Windows
Cinnamon Pecan Shortbread
Cranberry Pecan Shortbread Cookies
Gingerbread Cookies
Gingerbread Cookie Frosting
Legendary Chocolate Chip Cookies
Love Letters
Neiman Marcus Cookie Recipe
Orange Poppyseed Cookies
Peanut Butter Firecrackers
Peanut Blossoms
Royal Icing for Cookies
Swedish Cinnamon Cookies

Cherry Mocha Balls

Terri Grimes, Indianapolis Indiana

These are the Hubsters favorite cookie. They are the first cookie I make each holiday season and the first to disappear too.

1 cup butter

½ cup sugar

4 teaspoons vanilla

2 cups all purpose flour

¼ cup unsweetened cocoa

½ teaspoon salt

1 cup chopped pecans

2/3 cup maraschino cherries, chopped

1 ½ cups confectioners sugar

In medium bowl cream butter. Gradually add sugar and vanilla. Beat until light and fluffy. In separate bowl sift together flour, cocoa and salt. Gradually add flour mixture to butter mixture, mixing well. Stir in pecans and cherries. Chill dough approximately 1 hour for ease in handling. Preheat oven to 350°F. Shape dough into 1 inch balls and place on ungreased baking sheet 1 inch apart. Bake 12 to 15 minutes. When cool toss cookies in confectioners sugar. Store in an airtight container. Makes 6 dozen.

Chocolate Caramel Poppers

Brooke Houk, Schweinfurt Germany

1 cup butter	*1 teaspoon baking soda*
1 cup sugar	*2 teaspoons vanilla*
1 cup firmly packed brown sugar	*1 cup chopped pecans, divided*
2 eggs	*1 tablespoon sugar*
2 ¼ cups all-purpose flour	*One 9-ounce package chewy caramel candies, cut into halves*
¾ cup cocoa	

Preheat oven to 375°F. Beat butter until light and fluffy. Gradually add sugars, mixing well. Add eggs, beating well. Combine flour, cocoa, and soda. Add to butter mixture and mix well. Stir in vanilla and ½ cup of the chopped pecans. Cover the dough and refrigerate for 1 hour. Combine remaining ½ cup pecans and tablespoon of sugar, set aside. Remove dough from fridge. Gently press 1 tablespoon of dough around each caramel candy half, forming a ball. Dip one side of the cookie into sugar pecan mix and place pecan side up onto ungreased baking sheet and bake for 8 minutes. They will look too soft, but this is what you want. Let cool one minute on cookie sheet and then it's ok to move them to wire racks to cool.

Chocolate Chai Latte Cookies

Brooke Houk, Schweinfurt Germany

One 18.25-ounce box butter recipe chocolate cake mix

3 tablespoons instant Chai tea latte mix (or substitute 1 1/2 teaspoon ground cinnamon, 1 teaspoon ground cardamom, 1 teaspoon ground ginger and 1/4 teaspoon ground cloves)

1/2 cup butter, softened

1 egg

3 tablespoons milk

1 cup milk chocolate chips

DRIZZLE:

1 1/2 cup powdered sugar

1 1/2 teaspoons ground cinnamon

3-5 tablespoons water

Heat oven to 350°F. Combine all cookie ingredients except chocolate chips in large bowl. Beat at medium speed until well mixed and smooth. Stir in chocolate chips by hand. Shape dough into 3/4 inch balls. Place 2 inches apart onto un-greased cookie sheets. Bake for 9-11 minutes or until tops are set and cracked. Cool for 2 minutes; remove from cookie sheets to cool completely. Combine all drizzle ingredients except water in small bowl. Add enough water for desired drizzling consistency. Drizzle over cooled cookies. Allow drizzle to set for about 30 minutes and then store cookies between waxed paper with a tight fitting lid to stay fresh and moist.

Chocolate Pecan Pralines

Cindy Newsom, Walker Louisiana

Chocolate chips should be chilled. Assemble all the ingredients and utensils before starting to cook. (Measure out the chocolate chips and keep them refrigerated until just before needed.) You will also need a large, heavy-bottomed stainless steel pot or skillet with deep sides, a long-handled metal whisk or spoon, 2 large spoons (or an ice cream scoop with a manual release) and a very lightly greased cookie sheet.

3/4 cup unsalted butter	*1 cup coarsely chopped pecans*
1 cup granulated sugar	*2 cups whole pecan halves*
1 cup packed, light brown sugar	*2 tablespoons vanilla extract*
1 cup milk	*1 1/2 cups semisweet chocolate chips, chilled*
1/2 cup heavy cream	

Melt the butter in the pot over high heat; add the sugars, milk, cream and chopped pecans. Cook 5 minutes, whisking constantly. Reduce heat to medium, and continue cooking and whisking 10 minutes. Add the pecan halves and continue whisking and cooking until done, about 8 to 10 minutes. (If the mixture smokes excessively toward end of cooking time, lower the heat.) Stir in vanilla extract and immediately drop about 1/4 cup of chocolate chips into about one-sixth of the batter. Stir quickly and just enough to cover some of the chips with batter but not enough to allow the chips to melt. Quickly drop the chocolate mixture onto the cookie sheet by heaping spoonfuls, using the second spoon to push the batter off the first (or use ice cream scoop); each praline should be about 2 inches in diameter and 1/2 inch thick. Repeat with remaining mixture, stirring briefly before adding more chocolate chips. The cooled pralines should be light brown, opaque, somewhat chunky and crumbly.

Church Windows

Terri Grimes, Indianapolis Indiana

These are my daughters' favorite holiday cookies. Often I will leave these cookies unsliced and cut them into slices when company arrives.

1 stick butter, softened

One 12-ounce package semisweet chocolate chips

1 teaspoon vanilla extract

1 cup chopped walnuts

One 10 ½-ounce package mini marshmallows multi-color

2 cups flaked coconut, divided

In a large saucepan, melt the butter and chocolate chips over low heat until completely melted, stirring often. Cool the mixture for about 10 minutes, until cool but not to the point of hardening. Put marshmallows and nuts in a large bowl; stir in chocolate/butter mixture until marshmallows are well coated (but not melted). Tear two sheets of waxed paper (about 6 inches wide by 12-inch long) and sprinkle each generously with coconut. Divide dough into halves and spoon half of the mixture lengthwise down the center of a 12- inch piece of waxed paper. Shape into a 2" x 12" log. Wrap the log firmly in the waxed paper, folding the ends snugly. Then place in large plastic bag or saran wrap or foil, because you need to make sure it is airtight. Repeat with the other half of the marshmallow mixture and coconut. Refrigerate overnight. Unwrap each log and cut into 1/4 inch slices and serve.

Cinnamon Pecan Shortbread

Terri Grimes, Indianapolis Indiana

¾ cup butter

1 cup sugar

1 egg

1 teaspoon vanilla

1/8 teaspoon salt

1 cup finely shopped pecans

2 cups all-purpose flour

¼ cup sugar

1 tablespoon cinnamon

Cream butter. Gradually add sugar and beat until light and fluffy. Add egg, vanilla and salt, beating well until light and fluffy. Stir in pecans. With spoon stir in flour. Divide dough in half. Form each half into a log. Wrap each half in waxed paper or plastic film and chill approximately 1 hour for ease in handling. Preheat oven to 350°F degrees. Slice dough into ¼ inch slices and place on ungreased baking sheet 1 inch apart. Sprinkle each cookie with granulated sugar. Bake 10 to 12 minutes. Cool cookies on wire racks. When cool store in an airtight container.

Yield 3 dozen

Cranberry Pecan Shortbread Cookies

Terri Grimes, Indianapolis Indiana

I started off with a recipe from a friend for what she deemed as the "Worlds Best Christmas cookie". It was pretty darn good. But with a few changes and additions I think it is even better now. These cookies melt in your mouth. They are so good and buttery. They are the BEST cookie I have ever eaten in my life! I find that using the confectioners sugar and the cornstarch make them absolutely melt in your mouth.

1 1/4 cups butter, softened

1 cup confectioners/powdered sugar

2 cups all-purpose flour

1/4 cup cornstarch

1 cup dried cranberries

1 cup white chocolate chips

1/2 cup chopped pecans

Preheat oven to 325°F. Cream butter and sugar until light and fluffy. Mix in the flour and cornstarch, a little at a time, until combined. Stir in dried cranberries, chips and pecans. Roll dough into 1-inch balls. Place 1 dozen at a time on ungreased cookie sheets. Flatten with your palm or the bottom of a glass or measuring cup. Bake 15 minutes. They will remain white, you do NOT want them to be browned. Remove from sheets and cool on wire rack.

Yield 6 dozen

Gingerbread Cookies

Terri Grimes, Indianapolis Indiana

This is my granddaughter, Jasmine's favorite Christmas cookie. She loves to help me bake them at Christmas time. Since this recipe makes so many cookies, quite often I will cut it in half. Also you can freeze half of the dough to use another time.

1 cup butter softened	*2 ½ teaspoons ground ginger*
1 cup sugar	*1 ½ teaspoons baking soda*
1 cup molasses	*1 ½ teaspoons ground cinnamon*
¼ cup water	*½ teaspoon ground allspice*
5 cups all-purpose flour	*¼ teaspoon salt*

In mixing bowl cream butter and sugar. Beat in molasses and water. Combine flour, ginger, baking soda, cinnamon, allspice and salt; gradually add to creamed mixture. Cover and refrigerate for at least 1 hour, or until easy to handle. On lightly floured surface roll out dough to ¼ inch thickness. Cut with cookie cutters that have been dipped in flour. Place 2 inches apart on un-greased baking sheets. Bake at 350°F for 10 to12 minutes. Remove from baking sheets and place on wire racks to cool. When cool, frost cookies with gingerbread cookie frosting.

Gingerbread Cookie Frosting

Terri Grimes, Indianapolis Indiana

I use this frosting to ice my famous Gingerbread Cookies. My granddaughter, Jasmine, loves to use my piping bags to draw skirts and dresses on the gingerbread ladies using this frosting.

1 pound confectioners sugar

¼ cup water

1 ½ teaspoons light corn syrup

½ teaspoon vanilla extract

In small mixing bowl combine frosting ingredients. Beat until smooth. At this point you can put some in small bowls and tint with food coloring. Use your frosting piping set to ice cookies or if you don't have one, place frosting in small bag, cut a small hole in the corner of the bag. Pipe frosting onto the cookies, or better yet let your Granddaughter frost them.

Legendary Chocolate Chip Cookies

Sharon Lehrer, Roseville California

My Mom found this recipe on the back of a cake mix box when my brother Bob was in the Army in the 1970's. Mom and I baked these cookies and brought them with us when he could have visitors for the first time. They were such a hit with Bob and all his army buddies that he always requested more. These cookies went all over the United States via the Army. I made such large cookies that instead of using a Pringles can to package them for shipping, I had to use a coffee can!

One 18 ½-ounce package yellow cake mix

One 12-ounce package semi-sweet chocolate chips

2 eggs

3/4 cup oil

Preheat oven to 350°F. In mixing bowl combine dry cake mix, eggs and oil. Mix well. Stir in chocolate chips. Drop tablespoons of dough onto greased cookie sheet, placing 2 inches apart. Bake 10-12 minutes. Cool on wire rack and enjoy.

Variation: Use chocolate cake mix instead of yellow and use peanut butter chips instead of the chocolate chips.

Love Letters

Brooke Houk, Schweinfurt Germany

2 cups all-purpose flour

½ teaspoon salt

¼ cup vegetable shortening

4 ounces cream cheese

½ cup sugar

1 large egg

1 egg yolk

1 teaspoon vanilla extract

¼ teaspoon lemon zest (optional)

Filling*

Preheat oven to 350°F. In medium bowl, whisk together flour and salt. Set aside. In large bowl, cream shortening, cream cheese and sugar until light and fluffy. Beat in egg, egg yolk, vanilla, and lemon zest. Gradually blend in the dry ingredients. On a lightly floured surface, roll out the dough to a thickness of 1/4 inch. Or you can put the dough on a sheet of parchment paper, and put a piece of plastic wrap on top. Roll the dough through the plastic wrap: it won't stick to the pin this way, and you can peel up the plastic and reposition it if you need to. Aim for a 12 by 15 inch rectangle. Using a sharp knife or a pizza cutter cut the dough into 3 inch squares. Place 1 inch apart onto an ungreased baking sheets. Drop a tsp of filling into the center of each square (if you put too much filling in it will spill out during cooking) and fold the corners up into the center like an envelope. Lightly seal the seams by pressing them together or pinching if necessary. Bake for 20 to 22 minutes or until lightly colored; not browned. Place on wire racks to cool fully.

***FILLING OPTIONS:** Peanut butter, chocolate chips, white chocolate, almond or pistachio paste, 3/4 cup cranberry jam, or apricot, strawberry, blueberry (just make sure that if you use jam you mix it up with 1 tablespoon flour or cornstarch)*

Neiman Marcus Cookie Recipe

Terri Grimes, Indianapolis Indiana

This was an emailed story, which turned out to be a hoax. The saga went that a woman went to a Neiman-Marcus Cafe and decided to try the "Neiman-Marcus cookie." It was so excellent that she asked for the recipe. The waitress said "no, but you can buy the recipe at only two fifty, it's a great deal!" The woman agreed and told her to put it on her credit card. When she received her VISA statement from she saw she had been charged $250.00 for the recipe. They refused to refund her money. So the woman said that she was going to send the recipe to every email address she could find and ask them to send it to everyone they knew as well. Ah, don't you just love Internet hoax's? I tried these cookies and they were pretty good. Not $250 worth of good, but good nonetheless. (I would recommend cutting the recipe in half unless you want to eat a lot of cookies).

2 cups butter	1 teaspoons salt
2 cups granulated sugar	2 teaspoons baking powder
2 cups packed brown sugar	2 teaspoons baking soda
4 eggs	24-ounces chocolate chips
2 teaspoons vanilla extract	One 18-ounce Hershey Bar, grated
5 cups oatmeal	3 cups chopped nuts, your choice
4 cups all-purpose flour	

Preheat oven to 375°F. Cream together butter and sugars. Beat eggs and vanilla into creamed sugars until light and fluffy. Combine oatmeal, flour, salt, baking powder, and baking soda. Slowly beat dry mixture into wet mixture. Stir in chocolate chips, grated chocolate, and nuts. Roll dough into 1" balls and place 2" apart on an ungreased cookie sheet. Bake 10 minutes. Cool on wire racks.

Yield 3 dozen

Orange Poppyseed Cookies

Terri Grimes, Indianapolis Indiana

¾ cup butter	2 cups all-purpose flour
1 egg	2 tablespoons poppy seeds
1 teaspoon vanilla	½ teaspoon orange extract
1/8 teaspoon salt	½ cup sugar for garnish

Cream butter. Gradually add sugar and beat until light and fluffy. Add egg and vanilla, poppy seeds, salt and orange extract, beating well until light and fluffy. With spoon stir in flour. Divide dough in half. Roll each half into a log. Form each half in waxed paper or plastic film and chill approximately 1 hour for ease in handling. Preheat oven to 350°F. Slice dough into ¼ inch slices and place on ungreased baking sheet 1 inch apart. Sprinkle each cookie with granulated sugar. Bake 10 to 12 minutes. Cool cookies on wire racks. When cool store in an airtight container.

Yield 3 dozen

Peanut Butter Firecrackers

Brooke Houk, Schweinfurt Germany

One 18-ounce package refrigerated
sugar cookie dough

6 tablespoons all-purpose flour

4 tablespoons creamy peanut butter

1 cup semisweet chocolate chips

½ cup colored sprinkles or chopped
peanuts

Preheat oven to 350°F. Remove dough from wrapper. Let dough stand at room temperature for about 15 minutes. In bowl combine flour, dough and peanut butter. Beat at medium speed with electric mixer until well blended. Wrap dough in plastic wrap and refrigerate approximately 1 hour to chill dough for ease in handling. Roll dough into 1-inch balls. Place on un-greased cookie sheet about 2 inches apart (I recommend using parchment paper). Bake 7-10 minutes or until set. Cool on wire rack. While cookies are cooling, melt your semisweet chocolate. I melt mine in the microwave in 30-second intervals. Be careful not to burn chocolate. Once cookies are cool, dip tops of cookies into melted chocolate and place on wax paper. Sprinkle tops of cookies with sprinkles (or chopped peanuts) and allow chocolate to set (about 30-60 minutes). Yum!

Yield 3 dozen

Peanut Blossoms

Terri Grimes, Indianapolis Indiana

This is one of the many cookies I make for the holidays each year. They are the perfect cookie for granddaughters to help with by pressing the kisses in the center of each cookie. A variation I have tried is to press miniature peanut butter cups in the center of each cookie instead of a Hershey's kiss. Those are great too!

48 Hershey's Kisses Chocolates	*1 egg*
1/2 cup butter, softened	*1 teaspoon vanilla extract*
½ cup creamy Peanut Butter	*1 ¾ cup all-purpose flour*
½ cup sugar	*1 teaspoon baking soda*
½ cup packed light brown sugar	*Extra sugar for topping*

Heat oven to 375°F. Remove wrappers from chocolates. Beat butter and peanut butter in large bowl until light and fluffy. Add ½ cup sugar and brown sugar; beat until fluffy. Add egg and vanilla; beat well. Stir together flour, baking soda and salt; gradually beat into peanut butter mixture. Shape dough into 1-inch balls. Roll in extra granulated sugar; place on ungreased cookie sheet. Bake 8 minutes. Immediately press a chocolate into center of each cookie; cookie will crack around edges. Return to oven for 2 more minutes. Cool on wire rack.

Yield 4 dozen

Royal Icing for Cookies

Terri Grimes, Indianapolis Indiana

I use this icing on Sugar cookies. This icing dries hard so that makes it the perfect frosting for holiday sugar cookies.

3 tablespoons meringue powder   *6 tablespoons warm water*

1 pound sifted confectioners sugar

Using an electric mixer beat meringue powder and confectioners sugar warm water until icing forms peaks (7 to 12 minutes). I separate frosting in small batches and tint each batch a different color. Be sure to use food coloring paste, not liquid food coloring. Liquid food coloring will thin your frosting.

Yield 3 cups

Swedish Cinnamon Cookies

Terri Grimes, Indianapolis Indiana

Many years ago I had a grumpy postman. I started baking him these cookies once a week and suddenly he was the nicest, sweetest postman I have ever encountered.

2/3 cup butter	*1 teaspoon baking powder*
1 cup sugar	*1 teaspoon cinnamon*
1 egg	*½ cup finely chopped walnuts*
1 teaspoon vanilla	*2 tablespoons cinnamon*
1 1/3 cup all-purpose flour	*2 tablespoons sugar*

Cream butter. Gradually add sugar, beating until fluffy. Beat in egg and vanilla. In small bowl combine flour, baking powder and cinnamon. Stir flour mixture into butter/sugar mixture until incorporated. Cover and chill 30 minutes. Meanwhile make topping by combining walnuts, 2 tablespoons cinnamon and 2 tablespoons sugar in small bowl. Roll chilled dough into small 1-inch size balls. Roll each ball into topping. Place dough ball on ungreased cookie sheet 2 inches apart. Bake in preheated oven at 350°F for 10 to 12 minutes.

Yield 3 dozen

Desserts

Banana Pudding

Bird's Nests

Butterfinger Ice Cream

Chocolate Philly Fudge

Christmas Holly

Hershey's Homemade Chocolate Ice Cream

Key Lime Tarts

Never the-Same-Twice Almond Float

Nutty Peach Crisp

Mamie Eisenhower's Million Dollar Fudge Recipe

Marshmallow Krispie Cakes

Melty Mints

Melty Mints Butter Flavored

Molten Lava

One Bowl Brownies

Peanut Butter and Jelly Bars

Smooth as a Redneck

Strawberry Pretzel Salad

Tootsie Rolls

Banana Pudding

Terri Grimes, Indianapolis Indiana

This is a wonderful banana pudding recipe that went around the Competition BBQ circles several years ago. Pudding wars broke out as each team tried to make the mother of all banana puddings. In the end, after the smoke cleared, this recipe reigned supreme. Hail to the pudding!

Two 1-pound bags Pepperidge Farm Chessmen cookies

6 bananas, peeled and sliced

2 cups milk

One 5-ounce box instant French vanilla pudding

One 8-ounce package cream cheese, softened

One 14-ounce can sweetened condensed milk (not evaporated)

One 12-ounce container Cool Whip, thawed

Line the bottom of a 13x9-inch dish with 1 bag of cookies and layer bananas on top. In large bowl, combine the milk and pudding mix. Beat on low for 1 minute with an electric mixer. In separate bowl combine cream cheese and condensed milk, beating until smooth and creamy. Fold Cool Whip into cream cheese mixture. Fold cream cheese mixture into pudding mixture until well blended. Pour the mixture over the cookies and bananas. Cover pudding with the remaining bag of cookies. Refrigerate at least two hours. My personal option is to cover pudding with meringue instead of the 2nd bag of cookies. Just use your favorite meringue recipe and stick under the broiler for a minute or two until the meringue is lightly browned. Then refrigerate to set pudding.

Serves 12

Bird's Nests

Brooke Houk, Schweinfurt Germany

One 5-ounce can chow mien noodles

One 7-ounce bag flaked coconut

One 12-ounce bag butterscotch chips

Assorted candies to put on top

Sauté coconut in nonstick skillet until lightly browned. Be careful not to burn. Microwave butterscotch chips 1 minute, stir and microwave 15 seconds more or until chips are melted. Mix chow mien noodles, coconut and melted butterscotch chips. Form into birds nests shapes and let sit for 1 hour or until hardened. Decorate with assorted candies like jellybeans and foil wrapped chocolate eggs.

Butterfinger Ice Cream

Julie Cameron, Des Moines Iowa

2 cups sweetened condensed milk

3/4 cup smooth peanut butter

6 cups whole milk

1 pint heavy whipping cream

Six 2.1-ounce Butterfinger candy bars

Stir condensed milk and peanut butter together until smooth. Mash Butterfinger bars until mixture is crumb consistency. Add milk and whipping cream, and pour into ice cream freezer. If not to fill-line, add more milk. Freeze according to manufacturer's directions.

Yields 6 quarts

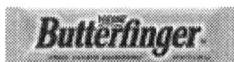

167

Chocolate Philly Fudge

Terri Grimes, Indianapolis Indiana

One 8-ounce package cream cheese, softened

4 cups sifted powdered sugar

Four 1-ounce squares unsweetened baking chocolate, melted

½ cup chopped walnuts

1 teaspoon vanilla

Beat cream cheese in large bowl on medium speed until fluffy. Gradually add sugar, beating until well blended. Add remaining ingredients, mixing well. Spread into greased8-inch square pan. Refrigerate several hours or until firm. Cut into 1-inch squares to serve.

Christmas Holly

Terri Grimes, Indianapolis Indiana

This is a fun recipe for kids to help make. Be warned that you will end up with green hands though. We like to shape the "holly" into Christmas wreaths sometimes. It makes a great holiday presentation.

½ cup (1 stick) butter

30 large Marshmallows

1 to 1 ½ teaspoons Green food coloring

4 1/2 cups Cornflakes

½ cup red hot candies (optional)

Melt together margarine and marshmallows. Add 1 to 1 1/2 teaspoon of food coloring. Add cornflakes. Drop by spoonful on waxed paper. Sprinkle with sprinkles and/or decorate with red hots. Let dry.

Hershey's Homemade Chocolate Ice Cream

Julie Cameron, Des Moines Iowa

5 eggs

1 cup sugar

Two 14-ounce cans condensed milk

6 cups Hershey's Chocolate Milk

1 1/2 teaspoons vanilla

3-ounces semi-sweet chocolate, melted

Beat eggs. Add sugar and mix well. Add condensed milk, chocolate milk, melted chocolate, and vanilla one ingredient at a time, stirring well after each addition. Mix until smooth. Pour directly into ice cream mixer or machine. For best results let ice cream freeze over night.

Yields 6 one-cup servings.

Key Lime Tarts

Terri Grimes, Indianapolis Indiana

24 Key Lime Cooler cookies

One 8-ounce package cream cheese, softened

1 egg

½ cup sugar

2 tablespoons Key Lime juice

1 teaspoon lime zest

Fresh sweetened whipped cream

Mint leaves or lime zest for garnish (optional)

Preheat oven to 350 degrees. Fill mini muffin tins with paper cups. Place 1 Key Lime Cooler cookie in the bottom of the cup, flat-side down. In large bowl combine cream cheese, egg, sugar, lime juice, and lime zest, beating until smooth and creamy. Fill the cupcake cups to the top. Bake 10 to 12 minutes. Remove tarts from pan to cool. When completely cool, fit a star tip in a pastry bag and fill with the whipped cream. Pipe the whipped cream on top of the tarts. Garnish with tiny mint leaves or lime zest.

Yields 24 tarts.

Never the-Same-Twice Almond Float

Bonita DelRey, Chicago Illinois

This warm weather dessert never fails to get oohs and ahhhs. Its names include Stanley's Almond Float, Fruit Stand Float, and Never the-Same-Twice Almond Float. The recipe's inspiration was Almond Dofu, a Chinese dessert. You'll find it best to assemble the dessert no more than 2–4 hours before serving. Keep refrigerated for best results.

1 tablespoon unflavored gelatin

2/3 cup cold water

2 tablespoons sugar

¼ teaspoon five spice powder

2/3 cup boiling water

2/3 cup milk or evaporated milk

1 1/2 teaspoons almond extract

2–3 drops food coloring (optional)

5 or more cups of mixed fresh fruits such as strawberries, raspberries, blueberries, blackberries, kiwi, mango, papaya, peaches, grapes, pitted cherries, watermelon

1/2 cup jicama cut in small squares or diamonds

1 Joya striped coconut candy bar, cut into small cubes. (Optional)

sliced or slivered almonds (Optional)

Pour the gelatin over the cold water and allow to soften for a few minutes. Add the sugar and five spice powder to the boiling water and stir to dissolve sugar. Stir in the evaporated milk. Add the softened gelatin mixture and stir in the almond extract and desired food coloring. Pour into an 8 or 9-inch square pan. Chill until firm. Slice strawberries in half. Leave remaining berries whole. Cut remaining fruit into berry sized pieces. Layer fruit in clear, straight sided bowl. Place particularly ripe berries on the bottom to create a natural berry syrup. Place firmer fruit in bottom layers, more fragile fruit in upper layers, reserving raspberries and blackberries for the top layer. Sprinkle jicama throughout layers. Cut firm gelatin mixture into shapes similar to jicama. Strew over top fruit layer. Add additional toppings as desired. Mix gently after presentation.

Serves 8 to 10

Nutty Peach Crisp

Terri Grimes, Indianapolis Indiana

Don't tell your guests how easy this dessert is. They will think you spent hours in your kitchen making this dish. It's really good served still warm and with a scoop of vanilla bean ice cream on top.

One 29-ounce can sliced peaches (do not drain)

One 18-ounce package Butter Pecan cake mix

½ cup butter, melted

1 cup flaked sweetened coconut

1 cup chopped nuts (pecan or walnuts work best)

Preheat oven to 325°F. Pour the can of peaches, with their juice, evenly over the bottom of a 13x9-inch baking dish. Sprinkle dry cake mix over peaches. Drizzle melted butter over cake mix. Sprinkle coconut over cake mix and butter. Top concoction with a sprinkling of chopped nuts on top. Bake 55 minutes. Allow to rest 15 minutes before serving.

Serves 8

Mamie Eisenhower's Million Dollar Fudge Recipe

Terri Grimes, Indianapolis Indiana

4 1/2 cups sugar

2 tablespoons butter

Pinch of salt

One 12-ounce can evaporated milk

One 12-ounce package semi-sweet chocolate chips

12-ounces German sweet chocolate

1 pint marshmallow cream

2 cups nuts (optional)

Boil the sugar, salt, butter and the evaporated milk together for 6 minutes. Put chocolate bits, German chocolate, marshmallow cream and nuts in a bowl. Pour the boiling syrup over the ingredients. Beat until chocolate is all melted, then pour in a pan. Let stand for a few hours before cutting. Remember it is better the second day.

Serves 14

Marshmallow Krispie Cakes

Brooke Houk, Schweinfurt Germany

One 9-ounce package toffees

4 tablespoons butter

3 tablespoons milk

1 cup marshmallows

6 cups rice krispies (I like to use cocoa krispies to kick it up a bit)

Lightly brush a 8x13 inch roasting pan with a little oil. Put the toffees, butter and milk in a saucepan and heat gently, stirring until the toffees have melted. Add the marshmallows and cereal; stir until well mixed and the marshmallows have melted. Spoon into the prepared roasting pan, level the surface and allow to set. Cut into squares, put into paper baking liners and serve. When cool and hard, cut into squares, remove from the pan and put into paper cases to serve.

Melty Mints

Terri Grimes, Indianapolis Indiana

One 3-ounce package cream cheese   *3 drops peppermint oil*

2 ½ cups confectioners sugar   *Food coloring as desired*

Mix all ingredients with hands until well combined. Fill candy molds with mint mixture. If you don't have a candy mold you can make small balls and flatten with fork. Keep mint in mold approximately 4 hours. Remove from mold and enjoy.

Yield 6 dozen.

Melty Mints Butter Flavored

Terri Grimes, Indianapolis Indiana

1 pound confectioners sugar   *¼ teaspoon peppermint oil*

¼ cup butter, softened   *Food coloring as desired*

2 tablespoons warm water

Mix all ingredients with hands until well combined. Fill candy molds with mint mixture. If you don't have a candy mold you can make small balls and flatten with fork. Keep mints in mold approximately 4 hours. Remove from mold and enjoy.

Molten Lava

Brooke Houk, Schweinfurt Germany

What could be better than a chocolate cake for dessert? How about a chocolate cake that is served warm with a river of chocolate running from it. This recipe is better than any dessert you can get in a restaurant.

½ cup (1 stick) butter, melted	*6 tablespoons flour*
Four 1-ounce squares semisweet baker's chocolate	*2 eggs*
	2 egg yolks
½ teaspoon almond extract	*Whipped cream or ice cream (optional)*
½ cup powdered sugar	

Preheat the oven to 425. Lightly grease four 4-ounce custard cups. In double boiler or microwave, melt chocolate and butter. Stir in sugar. In a small bowl, lightly beat eggs. Add some chocolate mixture to eggs to temper eggs. Carefully, stir egg mixture into chocolate mixture. Add flour and combine completely. Stir in almond extract. Pour batter into custard cups. Place them on baking sheet and bake for 13-15 minutes. Centers should be soft but sides should be done. Run a knife carefully around the edges, then invert cups on individual serving plates. Remove cups and serve immediately otherwise the chocolate "lava" won't spill out. This is fabulous on it's own but even better served with whipped cream or ice cream.

Serves 4

One Bowl Brownies

Terri Grimes, Indianapolis Indiana

Four 1-ounce squares unsweetened chocolate

3/4 cup (1 1/2 sticks) butter

2 cups sugar

3 eggs

1 teaspoon vanilla

1 cup flour

1 cup coarsely chopped nuts (optional)

Preheat oven to 350°F. Grease bottom of 13X9-inch pan. Line pan with parchment paper. Grease paper. Microwave chocolate and butter in large bowl on high 2 minutes or until melted. Stir sugar into chocolate mixture until well blended. Mix in eggs and vanilla until well blended. Stir in flour and nuts until well blended. Spread in prepared pan. Bake for 30 minutes. Do NOT over bake. Cool in pan 15 minutes. Lift out of pan onto cutting board. Cut into squares.

Yields 24 brownies

Peanut Butter and Jelly Bars

Kate Chaplin, Indianapolis Indiana

1 cup (2 sticks) unsalted butter, room temperature

3 cups all-purpose flour

1 ½ cups sugar

2 large eggs

2 ½ cups smooth peanut butter

1 ½ teaspoons salt

1 teaspoon baking powder

1 teaspoon pure vanilla extract

1 ½ cups grape jelly, or other flavor

2/3 cup salted peanuts, roughly chopped

Preheat oven to 350°F. Grease a 9x13 inch pan with butter and line the bottom with parchment paper. Grease the parchment and coat inside of pan with flour; set aside. Mix butter and sugar in a bowl. Beat until fluffy. Add eggs, peanut butter; beat until combined. Whisk together salt, baking powder and flour. Combine to previous mixture. Add vanilla extract. Transfer two-thirds of mixture to prepared pan. Spread evenly with offset spatula. Using offset spatula, spread jelly on top of peanut butter mixture. Dollop remaining third of peanut butter mixture on top of jelly. Sprinkle with peanuts. Bake until golden brown, about 45 minutes. Transfer to wire rack to cool, cut into about thirty-six 1 ½ by 2 inch pieces.

Yield 3 dozen

Smooth as a Redneck

Julie Cameron, Des Moines Iowa

One 3-ounce package instant vanilla pudding

One 14-ounce can sweetened condensed milk

1/2 cup sugar

1 gallon milk

Mix first three ingredients with about half the milk using an electric mixer. Stir in enough of the remaining milk to fill ice cream freezer. Freeze according to manufacturer's instructions. For variety: add one cup sweetened and chopped strawberries and one small strawberry Jell-O or use peaches with peach Jell-O.

Strawberry Pretzel Salad

Terri Grimes, Indianapolis Indiana

2 1/4 cup pretzels, crushed

4 tablespoons sugar

¾ cup (1 1/2 sticks) butter, melted

One 8-ounce package cream cheese

1 cup sugar

8-ounces Cool Whip, thawed

One 6-ounce package strawberry Jello

2 cups boiling water

Two 10-ounce packages frozen strawberries, thawed

Preheat oven to 350°F Combine crushed pretzels, 4 tablespoons sugar and melted butter. Press in the bottom of a 13x9 pan. Bake 15 minutes. Meanwhile mix cream cheese, 1-cup sugar and Cool Whip until creamy. Spread on cooled pretzel crust. Combine strawberry Jello, boiling water, and frozen strawberries. Refrigerate 15 to 20 minutes to congeal slightly. Pour on top of cream cheese mixture. Refrigerate until jello is set.

Serves 8 to 10

Tootsie Rolls

Terri Grimes, Indianapolis Indiana

1-ounce square unsweetened chocolate

1 tablespoon butter

1/4 cup dark corn syrup

1/2 tsp. vanilla

1-1/3 cups sifted powdered sugar

6 tablespoons instant nonfat milk powder

Place chocolate and butter in 4-cup glass measuring cup with a handle. Microwave, uncovered, at high power for at least 1 minute, stirring once during cooking time, until chocolate is melted. Stir in corn syrup and vanilla. Mix in sugar and milk powder. Knead with hands and make into rolls. Wrap in twists of waxed paper to store.

Misc.

Artic Rock Garden

Bubbles

Cinnamon Ornaments

Firewater

Pan Paint

Playdough

Rovers Rewards

Shake and Bake Mix

Weed-killer from Kitchen Ingredients

Wild Elephant Stew

Artic Rock Garden

Terri Grimes, Indianapolis Indiana

This is a wonderful summer activity for kids. Mine would eagerly run to the rock garden every morning to see what changes had occurred overnight.

1-inch rocks

4 tablespoon salt

4 tablespoons water

Food coloring

1 aluminum pie plate

4 tablespoons bluing – I use Little Boy Blue

1 tablespoon household ammonia

Scrub and dry the rocks. Place in pie plate. In bowl combine salt, water and bluing, stirring until the salt dissolves. Add ammonia and stir again. Pour mixture slowly over rocks, covering all surfaces. Place in a sunny dry spot. Drop food coloring in spots to add color. Watch your colorful rock garden grow.

Bubbles

Terri Grimes, Indianapolis Indiana

¼ cup Dawn dish liquid

½ cup water

1 teaspoon sugar

Combine all ingredients. Pour in plastic container or old bubble containers. This mixture keeps indefinitely and makes awesome bubbles!

Cinnamon Ornaments

Cindy Newsom, Walker Louisiana

This special recipe makes wonderful cinnamon-scented ornaments. (Do not eat!)
You can even write a message on them when they are still damp.

¾ cup cinnamon	*1 tablespoon ground nutmeg*
1 tablespoon ground allspice	*1 cup applesauce*
2 tablespoons ground cloves	*1 ½ tablespoons white glue*

In a bowl, mix cinnamon, allspice, cloves and nutmeg. Add in applesauce and mix
well. Pour in white glue and mix well until the mixture is stiff. Between two sheets
of waxed paper, roll out the dough to a 1/4-inch thickness. Use cookie cutters to cut
out the ornaments. Using a drinking straw, poke a hole in each one for hanging.
Allow several days to dry at room temperature. When dry, insert a ribbon in the
hole in each heart. Hang anyplace you wish to fill with the spicy aroma of
cinnamon.

Firewater

Terri Grimes, Indianapolis Indiana

In the spring I go overboard planting hot peppers since they are one of the few things that grow well for me. Thus, I end up being overrun with hot peppers in the summer. What better way to use them then make your own hot pepper sauce! Once you try this recipe you'll never have to buy hot sauce again.

12 cayenne chilies, stems removed	*½ cup white wine vinegar*
2 garlic cloves	*1 cup water*
½ yellow onion	*1 teaspoon salt*
½ lemon, juiced	*1 teaspoon sugar*

Place all ingredients in a heavy saucepan. Slowly bring to a simmer over medium heat. Simmer 20 – 30 minutes. Remove from heat and cool slightly. Pour the entire mixture into a blender or food processor and puree until smooth. Press the hot sauce through a mesh strainer lined with cheesecloth. Bottle and enjoy.

Pan Paint

Terri Grimes, Indianapolis Indiana

This makes a 'paint' similar to PAM. The only thing you are missing is the spray-can. This mixture keeps indefinitely.

½ cup flour   *½ cup shortening*

½ cup vegetable oil

Combine all ingredients together, mixing well until smooth. Store in a plastic container in your cupboard. Use a pastry brush to coat cake plans, pie plates, muffin tins, etc.

Playdough

Terri Grimes, Indianapolis Indiana

Kids love to make this Playdough almost as much as they enjoy playing with the actual Playdough.

1 cup flour   *Few drops food coloring*

½ cup salt   *1 tablespoon oil*

¼ cup water

Drop food coloring into water. In medium bowl combine flour, salt and colored water. Knead with fingers until well combined. Add oil. Mix well. When kids are finished playing with this Playdough make sure you put it in a plastic bag so it won't dry out.

Rovers Rewards

Terri Grimes, Indianapolis Indiana

Nothing says love better than homemade doggie biscuits for your pooch. These are so easy to make and a good project for little hands to help with.

¾ cup hot water	*2 teaspoons sugar*
½ cup margarine	*1 egg beaten*
½ cup powdered milk	*3 cups wheat flour, sifted*
½ teaspoon salt	

Preheat oven to 350. In a large bowl pour hot water over margarine. Stir in powdered milk, salt, sugar and egg. Add flour, ½ cup at a time, mixing well. Knead 3 to 4 minutes, adding more flour if necessary to make a soft dough. Pat or roll to ½-inch thickness. Cut with cookie cutter. Place on greased cookie sheet. Bake 50 minutes. Allow to cool and dry hard before giving to your pet. Store in covered container.

Shake and Bake Mix

Terri Grimes, Indianapolis Indiana

This stuff is great. I use it to coat not only chicken, but pork chops and even potato wedges.

4 cups flour	*2 teaspoons garlic powder*
4 cups cracker meal	*2 teaspoons onion powder*
4 teaspoons salt	*3 tablespoons paprika*
2 tablespoon sugar	*¼ cup oil or melted butter*

Preheat oven to 375°F. Mix all ingredients except cooking oil. Brush oil or butter on chicken parts. Coat with your homemade Shake and Bake. Bake 45 – 60 minutes or until chicken is golden and juices run clear. The shake and bake mix will last 3 months in your pantry.

Weed-killer from Kitchen Ingredients

Cindy Newsom, Walker Louisiana

We put it on very large weeds and they turned black but were not dead. It may require several applications depending on the size and type of weeds. Since I used 5% vinegar I would have had better success using a higher % vinegar. Also we sprayed it on Friday June 29th and went on vacation until July 9th. We were told that it started raining on Saturday July 1st and rained almost the whole week that we were gone. That may have affected the weed killer's ability to kill the entire plant.

1 gallon of vinegar*

1 cup of salt

8 tablespoons Dawn dish detergent (has to be Dawn)

Mix all ingredients together. Pour into a spray bottle and spray those pesky weeds away.

*Instructions call for the highest % solution vinegar for the best results. The higher the % of solution the better it works.

**Like everything else, there are negatives to using this. This Weed killer is nonselective; it will kill everything that it comes in contact with. Also prolonged" use can change the composition of the soil for years and can even make the soil sterile. These ingredients stay behind in the soil after the weed is dead. Vinegar breaks down the soil and salt changes the composition.

Wild Elephant Stew

Terri Grimes, Indianapolis Indiana

1 wild elephant   *2 rabbits (optional)*
Truck load of gravy

Cut elephant into bite sized pieces (takes about 3 weeks). Place in pot with gravy. Cook over medium heat 1 month. If more people show up, add 2 rabbits, but only in an emergency as most people object to having a *Hare* in their stew.

Serves a entire Village

Index

COOKIES

DESSERTS

MISC.

Recipe Contributors

I would like to extend my thanks and gratitude to my co-authors; those wonderful individuals who submitted recipes for this book. And we can't forget the brave, daring people who tested the recipes, to ensure that each and every recipe contained in this book is worthy of putting on your table and serving to your family.

Mabel Baker, Salisbury Maryland

Julie Cameron, Des Moines Iowa

Kate Chaplin, Indianapolis Indiana

Barbara Dahan, Berlin Maryland

Mark Danziger, Cayman Islands, Caribbean

Bonita DelRey, Chicago Illinois

Tammy Flowers, Hammond, Louisiana

Helen Giddings, Laurel Maryland

Greg Grimes, Indianapolis Indiana

Marion Grimes, Berlin Maryland

Terri Grimes, Indianapolis Indiana

Brooke Houk, Schweinfurt Germany

Linda Ilsley Topanga, California

Debra A. Kemp, Carmel Indiana

Sharon Lehrer, Sacramento California

Jennifer Macaire, Montchauvet France

Cindy Newsom, Walker Louisiana

Lottie Smith, Salisbury Maryland

Andrew Timmons, Indianapolis Indiana

Jasmine Timmons, Indianapolis Indiana

www.ingramcontent.com/pod-product-compliance
Lightning Source LLC
LaVergne TN
LVHW011349080426
835511LV00005B/206